Mount Rushmore

The Story of Mount Rushmore for 9-12-year-olds

(The History and Legacy of America's Most Unique Monument)

James Hubbell

Published By **Percy Clint**

James Hubbell

All Rights Reserved

Mount Rushmore: The Story of Mount Rushmore for 9-12-year-olds (The History and Legacy of America's Most Unique Monument)

ISBN 978-1-7781462-8-2

No part of this guidebook shall be reproduced in any form without permission in writing from the publisher except in the case of brief quotations embodied in critical articles or reviews.

Legal & Disclaimer

The information contained in this book is not designed to replace or take the place of any form of medicine or professional medical advice. The information in this book has been provided for educational & entertainment purposes only.

The information contained in this book has been compiled from sources deemed reliable, and it is accurate to the best of the Author's knowledge; however, the Author cannot guarantee its accuracy and validity and cannot be held liable for any errors or omissions. Changes are periodically made to this book. You must consult your doctor or get professional medical advice before using any of the suggested remedies, techniques, or information in this book.

Upon using the information contained in this book, you agree to hold harmless the Author from and against any damages, costs, and expenses, including any legal fees potentially resulting from the application of any of the information provided by this guide. This disclaimer applies to any damages or injury caused by the use and application, whether directly or indirectly, of any advice or information presented, whether for breach of contract, tort, negligence, personal injury, criminal intent, or under any other cause of action.

You agree to accept all risks of using the information presented inside this book. You need to consult a professional medical practitioner in order to ensure you are both able and healthy enough to participate in this program.

Table Of Contents

Chapter 1: National Heartbeats 1

Chapter 2: Art in America Should Be American 15

Chapter 3: Our Matchless Playground 29

Chapter 4: This Towering Wall 43

Chapter 5: Turn Them Jack Hammers On 54

Chapter 6: Double Whammy 66

Chapter 7: Heated Arguments and Conflicts 75

Chapter 8: A Shrine to Democracy 89

Chapter 9: The Creation of Rushmore 107

Chapter 10: Patriotism and Commercialism 121

Chapter 11: Construction And Logistics 133

Chapter 12: Controversies and Dissent 149

Chapter 13: Monumental Meaning . 163

Chapter 14: Modern Rushmore 176

Chapter 1: National Heartbeats

"We keep in mind the scale of national heartbeats are greater than village impulses, greater than nation desires or pursuits. Therefore we don't forget a rustic's memorial want to, like Washington, Jefferson, Lincoln and Roosevelt, have serenity, a Aristocracy, a power that reflects the gods who stimulated them and suggests the gods they have got come to be. As for sculptured mountains - Civilization, even its first-rate arts, is, maximum of it, amount-produced stuff: training, law, government, wealth - every is enduring only because the day. Too little of it lasts into tomorrow and the following day is pretty the enemy of in recent times, as in recent times has already all started out to overlook buried the day prior to this. Each succeeding civilization forgets its predecessor, and out of its frame builds its homes, its temples. Civilizations are ghouls. Egypt emerges as pulled apart with the resource of its successor; Greece changed into divided a number of the Romans; Rome became pulled to portions through the usage of bigotry and bitterness lots of which modified into engendered its very personal empire building." - Gutzon Borglum

Borglum

Generally talking, artists and engineers seemingly have little in common. Artists have a propensity to be loose spirits who live internal their minds, growing masterpieces top notch and small from ideas they dream up of their heads. Engineers, on the other hand, satisfaction themselves on practicality and their capacity to apply the device of technological know-how and motive to get a job completed. However, approximately 90 years in the past, art work and engineering met collectively at the side of a mountain in South Dakota to create one of the fine American landmarks of all time: Mount Rushmore.

The man within the again of the undertaking grow to be named Doane Robinson, however his feature might be overshadowed via that of the artist who designed it, the elaborate Gutzon Borglum. According to his daughter, Mary Ellis Vhay, Borglum "modified into so entire of power, I imply, it modified into a important pressure inside him, burning interior him. He can also want to appeal all people to do something if he honestly positioned his mind to it. And he can also decorate a terrible fuss if you did not." He modified into additionally bold and self-assured to the difficulty of vanity, predicting that when Mount Rushmore changed into finished, "[t]he dimensions of Washington's head may permit the Sphinx of Egypt to lie a number of the prevent of the nose and the eyebrow."

Robinson

As is frequently the case, Borglum's arrogance become certainly a cover that masked his very very very own emotions of loss of confidence and disappointment, numerous which stemmed lower lower back to his teenagers as the son of the second one accomplice in a polygamous Mormon family in Idaho. According to his granddaughter, Robin Carter, "There had been eight kids in the circle of relatives and there were higher halves at one time, and Gutzon's mom sincerely left the family and that they've been raised with the resource of the stepmother." Actually, Gutzon's mother didn't leave the family a lot due to the fact the family left her even as his father decided to transport to Nebraska, in which polygamy changed into illegal. Later, consistent with Vhay, Borglum "ran a long way from domestic because of the fact he turn out to be sad and at that, he started, I assume at the same time as he end up only 5 years antique, and he in the long run built up the self assurance inner himself that he may additionally need to do what he desired to do." John Houser, the son of considered one of Gutzon's assistants, brought, "He had a deep feel of his personal talents, I count on. He ran a ways from domestic some of instances to become an artist and wound up in California at a very early age reading art and he even stated he become going to be well-known earlier than he became 30."

At first, achievement seemed to elude Gutzon as he traveled backward and forward some of the United States and Europe, at the identical time as he continued honing his progressive competencies and searching for new commissions. During this time, he met and was mentored with the resource of Auguste Rodin, the famous French sculptor first-class recognized for his massive works of artwork. Then, his precise fortune modified. According to Carter, "He have become very distraught while he become in Europe and he did now not experience like he modified into making a living, he did now not revel in like he had a call for himself. He wasn't satisfied, and he favored to exchange all that. He desired to be, be diagnosed. ... In 1901 at the same time as he came decrease returned to the USA, he honestly burst into New York City shape of decided to become a very a achievement sculptor. And interior the ones first ten years he designed over a hundred portions for St. John the Divine in New York City, he'd sold the marble Lincoln for the Rotunda, he'd provided the Mares of Diomedes to the Metropolitan. He'd completed the Mackay statue in Reno, Nevada. He'd carried out Sheridan in Washington DC. I suggest in the first ten years, he turn out to be doing all this stuff."

Rodin

As his repute unfold, so did interest in his art work. According to Houser, "Every surely super artist has some thing of their character that they're able to impart into their paintings, this is precise and is best them. With Borglum I see the person as quickly as I contact the ones surfaces masses of time, I frequently anticipate almost to sense a hint glaze of strength it's far traversing throughout the shape. There's a life to it. There's a revel in of motion. And, I think that they had been finished typically right away and very rapid. My father said that regularly he would possibly are available in and do some factor much like this after which it might be done. Sometimes he have to truely have his match on and his Stetson, sporting his Stetson hat you comprehend, and he must are available and model for 15 mins and he would possibly say, "Cast it," you understand, and he'd stroll out. ... An artist has a wonderful many factors to artwork with, to create some issue aesthetic. You have the warmth and the coldness of colour. You have the smoothness and the roughness of texture. You have the assessment from mild and darkish. You additionally have at the equal time as you get to scale you discover that scale is a chic satisfactory in itself. In distinctive terms, whilst you notice some difficulty relatively huge, it has an effect on you actually as it's large."

In spite of his often virulent grievance in competition to American art and specially the u . S . A .'s monuments, Borglum seemed to apprehend what people wanted to peer. As he located it, "[Size] is emotional. There is a few factor in sheer quantity that awes and terrifies, lifts us out of ourselves." It changed into this perception that had been given him worried with the project to carve a four hundred x 1,500 foot bas-remedy on the aspect of a granite mountain in Georgia. According to Houser, "When Borglum become called all of the way right down to Stone Mountain to begin with, he become invited to do a small bust of Lee and positioned it on top of the mountain. And he counseled the Daughters of the Confederacy, he stated, placing a bust of Lee on pinnacle of that mountain may be like pasting a postage stamp on a barn door, you understand, it's miles incongruous. If you're going to speak about a mountain that period you have got to talk about a piece of sculpture it certainly is commensurate in a single way or every other. That shape of opened the door, I anticipate, to him for mountain carving."

As destiny can also need to have it, Borglum spent a decade of his existence on that venture only to be fired at the same time as the committee ran out of cash. At the same time, however, it positioned him inside the best location to take over the building of what could absolutely be his magnum opus, for it become an article approximately the Stone Mountain project that inspired Doane Robinson to gain out to Borglum about his non-public idea for a mountainside sculpture.

A contemporary photo of Stone Mountain

As the u . S . A . Historian for South Dakota, Robinson have become continuously seeking out methods to attract hobby to its splendor and sources, but he had a consistent problem attracting human beings to his country. He as quickly as admitted, "Tourists rapid get bored to death on environment except it has a few thing of unique hobby associated with it to make it great." In 1923, after seeing news about Stone Mountain, which modified into then being carved out of doors Atlanta, he predicted a comparable sculpture in his country. In 1924, he sent a telegram to Borglum that have a look at, "In the region of Harney Peak, within the Black Hills of South Dakota are opportunities for heroic sculpture of uncommon character. Would it's miles viable at the manner to format and supervise a big sculpture there? The idea has now not surpassed beyond the mere notion, but if or no longer it is viable that allows you to adopt the matter I enjoy quite high-quality we need to installation to finance such an business enterprise. I need to be glad to pay attention from you at your consolation."

Borglum modified into disturbing to find out a new undertaking, but he didn't need Robinson to recognize that, so he responded, "Very an lousy lot interested by your thought. Great scheme you have got have been given; hold to it; the North will welcome it. Am years in advance in my southern paintings can get to Black Hills inside the course of September."

Chapter 2: Art in America Should Be American

"Art in America need to be American, drawn from American assets, memorializing American fulfillment.... We see incoming ships loaded with the second-hand or counterfeit artwork of the antique international ... we see our town homes, our country and country wide homes, marked and counterfeited with the aid of the symbols of a human beings one thousand years vain.... Against this, all that is honest, all this is honest, revolts.... Those people who can come up with the coins for it thieve and beg and borrow the palms, the dress, the feelings of Greece and Rome ... we cling their rotting trophies on our walls, unaware of their starting location, unacquainted with their this means that, now not even sympathetic with the feelings that produced them. We have now not all started out to recognize that the topics we favored really— liberty of moral sense, freedom from European governments and from the stain of slavery have been matters to be satisfied with; that they'll be ours and that those gadgets by myself make us immortal; make us the envy of the arena. If we've were given art work of any type ... it need to write them in bold lines sooner or later of the pages of our records." - Gutzon Borglum

Over the subsequent 12 months, the men began raising cash and putting together plans for the task anticipated by way of the use of Robinson, but whilst Robinson had to start with alleged to commemorate crucial guys in South Dakota's statistics, Borglum had massive ideas and predicted a tribute to

George Washington and Abraham Lincoln that might draw human beings from in the course of the complete u . S . A .. It have emerge as best later that the imaginative and prescient stepped forward to four presidents with the addition of Thomas Jefferson and Theodore Roosevelt (the latter being a personal pal of Borglum himself). Borglum explained the idea for which includes those four: "The 4 American presidents carved into the granite of Mount Rushmore have been decided on...to commemorate the founding, boom, renovation and development of the us. They characterize the standards of liberty and freedom on which the country have become based. George Washington suggests the struggle for independence and the beginning of the Republic; Thomas Jefferson the territorial enlargement of the u . S .; Abraham Lincoln the everlasting union of the states and equality for all citizens; and Theodore Roosevelt, the 20th century function of the USA in global affairs and the rights of the commonplace man."

Once he arrived in Rapid City, Borglum went with Robinson on a excursion of the community geographical region, dotted as it have emerge as with the darkish mountains that gave the Black Hills their name. Finally, he determined the internet site he desired in Mount Rushmore, a massive upward thrust supplying a big, wide expanse that might supply him masses of room on which to carve his 30 story-tall faces. He referred to, "I was aware we were in some other worldwide ... and there a latest notion seized me— a belief that modified into to redirect me and dominate all my carving— the size of that mountain pinnacle! We seemed out over a horizon stage and beaten just like the rim of a high-quality cartwheel 2,000 feet beneath. We had reached upward toward the heavenly our bodies ... and it got here over me in an nearly terrifying way that I had never sensed what I changed into planning. Plans ought to alternate. The vastness I observed right right here demanded it." After finding the right spot, Borglum confided to his son, "Nothing but the Almighty can save you me from finishing this mission."

A picture of Mount Rushmore in advance than the mission

A image of the Black Hills from Mount Rushmore

Mount Rushmore may want to in all likelihood have clearly remained not anything greater than a mountain had Peter Norbeck now not taken an interest inside the project. Then a United States Senator but previously the Governor of South Dakota, Norbeck have become, within the terms of his grandson, Dr. Karl Wegner, "as hard because the Norwegian, northern pines, however additionally with the soul of an artist. His formal education come to be very confined, however somewhere in there he located the interest to pursue those greater highbrow and imaginative endeavors. He noticed this as an possibility to deliver people to the Black Hills. Any vacationers, any humans we may want to supply into South Dakota from the out of doors delivered their wallet, their dollars with them, and any out of doors dollars on this us of a that might be brought in have been desperately wanted."

Norbeck

In the autumn of 1924, Robinson wrote to Norbeck, "Borglum has come and lengthy past. I matter amount it one of the splendid reviews of my life to have spent days with someone of his genius and excessive character...He paid his very very very own prices for the adventure and talked like a person who've turn out to be high-quality of his ground...He said no longer something of his plans for financing besides that he came at the request of fellows deeply interested in a country huge memorial.... I can't often consider this awesome element is to be exceeded to us...Since the location is on the Forest Reserve ... federal regulations could be required and I instructed him you will appearance in the long run that is important in that course."

Norbeck proved to be Borglum's champion. According to Vhay, "He supported dad within the entirety. He were given very bypass with him at instances on the same time as dad might call for extra money and needed to have extra cash, however also I count on that Senator Norbeck modified proper into a bridge between dad and the local community." In early December 1924, Norbeck cabled the newly elected governor of South Dakota, "I expect this might be an opportunity to consistent one of the country wide factors of interest in this u.S.A. Of the united states of the highest innovative high-quality. I advise the united states of a appropriate 10000 bucks to be made available for research and surveys exceptional. It is an opportunity we should now not pass over."

Unfortunately, numerous the area people did now not need this kind of challenge, and one of the mission's most virulent warring parties turn out to be a girl named Cora Johnson. A writer for the Hot Springs Star, she in no way overlooked a risk to denigrate Robinson's plans, essential him on December 7, 1924 to put in writing down to her, "I prolonged inside the beyond located out no longer to argue with a girl. I most effective ask simply the manner you choice to justify yourself to posterity? The nice artist within the international has proposed to carry you the most majestic monument within the worldwide, and ye should now not."

In the early months of the 1925 united states congressional consultation in South Dakota, Robinson approached the legislature and asked for $10,000 seed cash to begin investment the task. However, it become a very awful time each politically and fiscally to make that request, and he grow to be soundly grew to grow to be down. Disappointed, Norbeck wrote to him approximately what modified into then referred to as the Harney Memorial, "To say that I am disgusted with the Gunderson manage is placing it mild. The defeat of the Harney Memorial appropriation makes me experience like "going off the reservation." The

Borglum rely seems to have come to a climax ... Borglum felt himself all-effective and did topics with a excessive hand [in Stone Mountain] ... His plans are not all sound, but he is a exceptional artist. I am in recent times in no temper of quitting: I revel in like combating all alongside the road ... I must make the politicians so darn plenty trouble they may be satisfied to attend to the park that allows you to have peace ... I am decided to tackle a actual combat."

Norbeck additionally called a press convention, during which he declared, "Borglum is one of the finest, if not the greatest, sculptors within the global ... He must command vast fortunes every year alongside collectively with his chisel ... But Borglum has reached the extent in life in which he desires to be in at the maximum essential undertaking of its type in the worldwide ... and to go away inside the again of him enormous works at the way to stand all the time."

While this could well were real, Borglum have become an extended way from the very extremely good guy to work with, as Norbeck himself changed into short mastering. Norbeck complained to Robinson, "This man works so rapid it's miles hard ... even to hold song of him ... He appears to take it without any consideration he goes to assemble the superb memorial and that there can be no hitch inside the application." At the identical time, Borglum changed into complaining that the venture grow to be not moving alongside speedy sufficient. He cabled to Norbeck, "I clearly have suggested actual motion continuously and brought the initiative as strongly as dignity permits.... Now I actually have proposed energy of will of stone determined, with historical rite, fuller plans, some checks this month, with government officiating. Possible cost of this, five thousand. Have talked with pals who ... assure me of guys who will provide the cash for Washington and Jefferson ... But we must devote this month even as public eye is ordinary on west. Personally haven't any goal of making any rate as sculptor, however preliminary actual fee need to be borne with the useful resource of South Dakotans or I can't do a little difficulty for you."

Nonetheless, the plans for what may also display to be the primary of severa dedications of the internet website online went ahead. On September 30, 1924, the Rapid City Journal proclaimed, "Rapid City folks that fail to wait the dedication of Rushmore will pass over ... the finest historic event which has ever happened inside the country. The carving of Rushmore is ... the most stupendous project of its kind in all facts. It is conceived with the aid of admittedly the amazing living sculptor.... It is epoch marking Every resident of Rapid City who can skip need to achieve this."

Chapter 3: Our Matchless Playground

"When God made our matchless playground, He did not intend that man need to

even in his wildest ravings dare to come with hammer, chisel,

block and deal with, pick out and mallet, to profane His age-vintage report,

to profane the face of Rushmore by means of manner of his puny, pygmy scratches.

Why have to man presume to modify the Creator's masterpieces,

wrought in everlasting granite, wrought via the use of forces so big

that no scientist can degree, that no human mind can draw near?

And to count on that guy, presumptive, need to deface and mutilate them!

Men and girls, 'tis your obligation to reinforce your earnest voices,

to the give up that all our human beings forthwith band themselves collectively

to keep from desecration finished merchandise from God's workshop

and positioned with the useful resource of manner of that Master-Artist within the playground of the Dakota." - John Tjaden, of the University of South Dakota, in 1925

On October 1, 1925, Borglum added in the front of a crowd of severa hundred people amassed on the foot of Mount Rushmore that he could quickly begin carving what he called the Great American Memorial. When finished, it would be bigger than the Statue of Liberty or maybe the Sphinx. As Vhay later positioned it, "If you begin manner over again while we first got here proper right here, my father became appeared upon as a weirdo, and a crank. They perception he changed into in reality surely very strange and he had massive thoughts that might cross nowhere."

Borglum had as soon as asserted no longer a few aspect can also moreover need to prevent him however God from making the undertaking, but it'd furthermore take a considerable amount of money to fund the challenge, and money may display to be a primary stumbling block. At the time, South Dakota became not intently populated and feature end up consequently now not prosperous, even though a exceptional deal greater like a territory than a country. Thus, even as Borglum delivered at a night meal following the primary willpower of the internet website that he desired $50,000 to begin the task, the businessmen in his target market have been no longer genuinely skeptical however angry. Furthermore, through manner of way of this time, Cora Johnson have become leading an more and more massive pressure in opposition to the project, calling it everything from fiscally irresponsible to environmentally suicidal. She and her fans were elevating a ruckus, and those who can also otherwise have donated to the carving had been listening.

Eventually, Borglum needed to loan his non-public domestic to elevate coins to start the undertaking, and he have emerge as having hassle making the minimal bills. In November 1925, he cabled Frank Hughes, president of the Rapid City Commercial Club (an organisation raising rate variety for the venture), "Can you twine me twelve to fifteen hundred bucks resulting from prices superior ... Actual fees chargeable to art work this year more than instances that however I don't count on to need it." To this, Hughes replied, "Much as would like to wire cash we haven't it handy. Senator Norbeck may be proper proper here on Thursday and could try hardest to get this completed."

Borglum's financial woes and innovative temperament would possibly live a trouble for every body round him, as Norbeck confessed to Hughes: "Frankly ... Mr. Borglum has been greater of a trouble to me this wintry climate than I ever anticipated. It has been now not feasible for me to get him to look the Black Hills aspect of the trouble. He modified into impatient due to the truth they did not ship him money in advance than he had ever rendered a bill. Then even as he determined out I grow to be not going to try and scare anybody in South Dakota, he labored round and had been given others to strive it ... He modified into desperately difficult-up and didn't understand which manner to show..."

Hoping to attraction to ego and the pocketbook of a wealthy donor with it, Robinson were given in touch with the man for whom Mount Rushmore become named. On December 14, 1925, he acquired the following records from Charles Edward Rushmore: "Late in 1883 the discovery of tin in the Black Hills become brought to the attention of a fixed of gentlemen in New York City and excited their hobby. I became a greater youthful attorney at the time, and became employed through way of those gentlemen early in 1884 to visit the Black Hills and steady options on the Etta mine, and distinct cassiterite places. My undertaking required me to stay numerous weeks inside the Hills, and to move back there on or 3 later sports in that 365 days and in 1885. Part of my time became spent among prospectors at Harney, and at a log cabin built in that community. In my lifestyles among those hard, however kindly, guys I conformed to their methods, and, can also I say it with becoming modesty, have turn out to be in select with them. I become deeply inspired with the Hills, and specifically with a mountain of granite rock that rose above the neighboring peaks. On one occasion whilst looking from close to its base, with nearly awe, at this majestic pile, I requested of the men who had been with me for its call. They said it had no name, but simply considered one in every of them spoke up and said 'We will call it now, and call it Rushmore Peak.' That come to be the start of the call it bears, and, as I have been informed, it's miles known as Rushmore Peak, Rushmore Mountain and additionally Rushmore Rock. Some time after the incident above narrated I actually have turn out to be informed that the call and identification of the Rock, or Mountain, modified into recorded within the Land Office in Washington at the instance of some of the good buddies stated, but I have in no way sought to verify this ft...this Rock is precise and lends itself admirably to a country wide monument of the kind you have advised. I consider you can reach wearing out the proposed layout."

At the same time, however, Robinson did now not get maintain of a take a look at. In truth, at some stage in the first year that Robinson campaigned for donations for the undertaking, he was only capable of increase $five,000. Borglum's popularity didn't help, with one Georgia newspaper maintaining, "Borglum is prepared to break another mountain. Thank God it is in South Dakota in which no individual will ever see it."

Even earlier than any carving might be achieved, the people had that lets in you to obtain the internet website, and to that surrender Borglum started out campaigning for the u . S . A . Government to begin building a road up the aspect of Mount Rushmore. This led then Governor William Bulow to bitch, "Almost every day he could probably call for that the road be constructed, and after every call for he anticipated the way to be completed earlier than breakfast the following morning. I mainly keep in mind one telegram he despatched me.... It became the longest telegram I ever obtained and it contained the most expressive language. There had been three hundred phrases in that telegram and Gutzon didn't repeat himself. Every phrase intended some thing. It have grow to be a masterpiece ... He said that he had without a doubt decrease decrease back from the mountain. That it had rained. That he had worn white get dressed footwear and a cutting-edge pair of white dress pants ... That he had ruined his shoes and his new white pants. I stressed him suggesting that the subsequent time he went to the mountain he want to placed on a couple of overalls and skip bare-footed. This advice held him down for severa days, however in a quick time he became lambasting again."

Bulow

By this time, there was a new motivation for building the road; Norbeck come to be now not quality a bridge among Borglum and the commonplace human beings, he changed into moreover a bridge maximum of the artist and effective human beings, collectively with President Calvin Coolidge. At Norbeck's invitation, "Silent Cal" decided to spend his summer season tour inside the Black Hills. Excited approximately having a president in their midst, the humans of South Dakota have been struck with a wild experience of patriotism and commenced donating to what they now taken into consideration Norbeck's mission. By the time, Coolidge arrived in South Dakota, the men have been able to kingdom with satisfaction that that they had raised $40 ,000 for the undertaking, impressing the president sufficient that he agreed to talk at a second strength of will rite planned for August 10, 1927.

However, in step with Borglum, an vital communication among him and Coolidge befell in advance than the speech. He later recalled, "President Coolidge whispered to me, 'Who's buying all this?' I stated, 'These farmers are identifying to buy it....' He stated, 'These humans cannot try this and that they ought not to be asked to do it ... You come see me once I get returned to Washington ... and we're able to set down and exercise session a plan ... [Norbeck] 'warned me to invite for the whole quantity. ... I did now not like that; I did no longer need to do it; and after I were given to Washington and talked with Mr. Coolidge he sent me proper over to [Treasury Secretary] Mellon. I noticed Mr. Mellon and went over the complete depend and advised him what I perception it might price [$

500,000].... He stated, 'What do you need us to do?' I said, 'I need half of of of the fee to be carried by using the Federal authorities and the rest through manner people.' He said, 'That isn't always honest to you.' 'Well,' I said, 'I want to get the human beings's enamel into this trouble.' [Then] Mr. Coolidge recommended me, 'Go to the Capitol and speak on your senators and installation a invoice ...' And that turned into all there has been to that."

Chapter 4: This Towering Wall

"We have come right here to dedicate a cornerstone that became laid via the hand of the Almighty. On this towering wall of Rushmore, within the coronary coronary coronary heart of the Black Hills, is to be inscribed a memorial with a purpose to represent some of the brilliant abilities of four of our Presidents, laid on thru the hand of a extremely good artist in sculpture. This memorial will crown the height of land the diverse Rocky Mountains and the Atlantic seaboard, wherein coming generations may view it all the time." - Calvin Coolidge at some point of the strength of will

After starting off his speech with a focal point at the assignment himself, Coolidge went directly to enumerate the wonderful inclinations of every of the guys to be represented on the hillside: "It is but herbal that any such layout must begin with George Washington, for with him starts offevolved offevolved that it is genuinely characteristic of America. He represents our independence, our Constitution, our liberty ... After our united states had been established, enlarged from sea to sea, and have grow to be devoted to famous authorities, the following tremendous challenge as to illustrate the permanency of our Union and to increase the precept of freedom to all population of our land. The draw close of this very fine accomplishment turned into Abraham Lincoln. Above all extraordinary country wide figures, he holds the love of his fellow countrymen. The artwork which Washington and

Jefferson started out, he prolonged to its logical quit ... That the thoughts for which those three guys stood might be even though greater firmly installation destiny raised up Theodore Roosevelt."

This brought him around to the problem on hand, and justifying why it become a splendid idea: "The union of those four Presidents carved at the face of the eternal hills of South Dakota will represent a noticeably country wide monument. It may be decidedly American in its idea, in its importance, in its meaning and altogether worth of our Country. No you can virtually look upon it understandingly with out figuring out that it's far a image of hope fulfilled. Its vicinity is probably full-size. Here in the heart of the continent, on the component of a mountain which likely no white guy had ever beheld within the days of Washington, in territory which became obtained via using using the motion of Jefferson, which remained an unbroken barren vicinity beyond the instances of Lincoln, which changed into especially favored with the useful resource of way of Roosevelt, the people of the destiny will see information and art work blended to portray the spirit of patriotism. They will understand that the decide of these Presidents has been positioned right proper here due to the fact via using following the truth they built for eternity. The essential ideas which they represented were wrought into the very being of our Country. They are steadfast as those ancient hills."

Finally, Coolidge concluded with each reward and a plea to the ones within the audience to maintain the first-rate work, and he supplemented it with a wonder pledge: "The people of South Dakota are taking the lead inside the education of this memorial out in their meager property ... Their strive and courage entitles them to the sympathy and assist of private beneficence and of the countrywide government. They apprehend fully that they've no method of succeeding in the development of their state besides a reliance upon American establishments. They do now not fail to understand their price. There isn't any power which could stay the improvement of this form of humans."

In spite of Coolidge's useful resource, as 1927 gave way to 1928, there has been but nowhere close to sufficient money to get the undertaking commenced, however this did now not save you Borglum, who rushed earlier on the idea that one way or the other the whole lot must exercise. Much to the chagrin of his combatants, he proved to be proper; whilst Congress got here decrease back into session after Christmas 1928, the legislators have been eventually ready to vote on some funding for the project. At the equal time, every person believed it grow to be critical to get the invoice handed in advance than Coolidge, a recognized supporter of the Rushmore undertaking, left place of business and have become changed via Herbert Hoover. Commission member William Williamson become concerned and confided to his diary:

"Feb. 18, 1929 Norbeck came over to the house numerous times in recent times to look me about the Rushmore bill. He fidgets like a aggravating girl because it's miles going the sluggish machine of adjustment in convention. Every hitch throws him into a chilly sweat. But for him I bet the assignment might have been dead extended in the past.

Feb. 21 To the comfort of absolutely everyone ... the conference report changed into in recent times disposed of with the useful resource of the House.

Feb. 22 The Senate agreed on the conference document.... The Senator may also additionally want to rarely incorporate himself with pride ... The venture now appears assured if the vagaries of the sculptor do not damage it."

Before Hoover end up inaugurated, the policies emerge as signed within the final days of Coolidge's time period. Known officially as Public Law 805 of the seventieth Congress, it decreed, "A charge is hereby created ... known as the Mount Rushmore National Memorial Commission ... to consist of twelve those who may be appointed via the President ... The charge is to complete the carving of the Mount Rushmore National Memorial, to embody heroic figures of Washington, Jefferson, Lincoln and Roosevelt, together with an entablature upon to be able to be reduce a appropriate inscription to be indicated via Calvin Coolidge.... Such memorial is to be built in keeping with designs and fashions thru Gutzon Borglum.... No fee shall ever be made for admission to the memorial grounds or viewing the memorial. Not multiple-half of the value of such memorial and landscaping shall be borne thru manner of the us, and not to exceed $ 250,000 is hereby prison for the cause ... The appropriate proportionate percent of the US could be advanced to stated fee sometimes ... to match the price range advanced from different belongings."

The very last phrase could display to be the maximum troubling throughout the task, as Norbeck, Borglum and others would need to keep to elevate matching price range for those furnished via the federal government. Understanding that no longer anything attracts investment like success, Borglum moved quickly to get began out, and he later described his method with the useful resource of manner of saying, "The one a success way to keep ... is to conform the sculptured bureaucracy to the existing stone formation, and not to transform the mountain into an architectural shape and then remodel the sculpture to in shape it. Sculptured art work on a mountain want to belong to the mountain as a natural a part of it; otherwise it turns into a hideous mechanical utility."

Recruiting the men he wished proved to be a high deliver of problem, because of the fact even the diverse many who have been seeking out jobs, few had any enjoy inside the sort of art work that would be required. Bob Hayes, whose father labored at the mountain, remembered, "It did no longer take too much training say to drill holes and so forth and run a jack hammer. It honestly took loads of guts, you will in all likelihood say. Some people went up there and labored someday, and I've been instructed, and that come to be all they preferred. They couldn't stand the peak and the dirt and so forth." Nick Clifford, who worked at the facet of the mountain, agreed, saying, "It became quite difficult in your first time going over there and putting in the bosun chair and try to punch holes in the granite. It took severa exercising. And you did now not get masses completed your first day, I'll tell you that. Most of the jack hammers weighed approximately forty or 50 kilos. And then you definitely without a doubt needed to carry your steel with you furthermore may also. So you had pretty a load occurring there. … Had they not come once more, there could be no Mount Rushmore as we're privy to it nowadays due to the reality Mr.

Borglum, it become no longer viable for him to teach a new group every three hundred and sixty five days. But those men were committed to the mountain. When the mountain may additionally close down for lack of cash or in the wintertime, that they had all should locate another venture. But at the equal time as the spring might possibly come spherical and they'll get the call to go back back, that they had cease what they were doing and come once more to paintings on the mountain."

Chapter 5: Turn Them Jack Hammers On

"The wind grow to be continuously a blowin' and it'd be quite gusty. The wind typically blew up there seems like. They changed into hangin' with a touch three-eighths inch cable. And that cable regarded quite small to me, to preserve them guys up there. And then that they had truly shake portions out of them when they'd flip them jack hammers on." - Glenn Bradford, a worker on Mount Rushmore

Working on Mount Rushmore modified into without a doubt an unforgettable revel in, as one employee recalled, "They gave me my jackhammer and they gave me my drills, and I went down over that mountain and stayed 'til midday. Then I went returned and stayed 'til night time. But, God! It scared me! No ways about it. But I did that for 3 or 4 days and, no foolin', I'd wake up inside the night time time time and grasp that vintage bed and hold close on for all I become definitely properly well worth, thinkin' I become fallin' off that mountain. Somehow you in no manner had any faith in that cable, and you can appearance down and word simply in which you'd fall to, and it regarded so damned a ways! So I advised Mr. Denison, "God! I honestly can't do this! I can't sleep at night time and I'm scared to loss of life hangin' available on that dinky cable." So he supply me a distinct interest and I stayed at Rushmore until it have emerge as finished."

Pictures of humans carving Washington's face

The first confronted carved changed into that of Washington. The guys used explosives to blast away part of the granite facet of the floor and have been pleased to look that, while the smoked cleared, there was a robust rock oval left in the back of that would become the face of America's first president. Meanwhile, Borglum had finished a scale version of his deliberate introduction in his studio, and what most people should in no manner recognize end up that his particular format called for a waist-up bust of each of the presidents. John Houser later described, "In doing a big piece of sculpture one of the issues of course is the enlarging. You're seeking to find factors in vicinity, and at one scale and then you definitely try to find the ones equal factors in place at each other scale. So what they did is, you have got a beam coming without delay out from a point that activates a swivel, and you may word the ranges at which it's miles turned, and in order you turn the simplest on the little model and you can say it's miles off 30 levels off to the right and it is out such masses of measurements and down so far after which in to this point, and you could find out a specific point on Washington's cheek for instance. So then you can do the equal element up at the mountain."

Picture of the model for Mount Rushmore

Red Anderson became out of exertions and out of coins whilst he signed as loads as artwork on Rushmore. He later said, "At first, Rushmore turn out to be in reality a few exceptional hobby and a loopy sort of a task at that. It have become sincerely a place to earn some cash and no longer some thing greater … But the longer we had been there, the more we began out to sense that we had been building a truly incredible trouble, and after some time anybody vintage arms have turn out to be actually committed to it." He additionally met and favored Borglum, as maximum of the guys did. Anderson said of him, "He become operating at the models of Rushmore, and the number one trouble that struck me have become how active the fellow changed into. The models had been in all likelihood ten feet immoderate and he needed to paintings on 'em from a ladder. But at the same time as he came down off that ladder he didn't climb down— he jumped. He wasn't the form of man you'd 'true day' and begin speakme to. You waited till he started talkin' to you. So inside the starting I virtually noticed him and that have emerge as all. Then, one day he determined the Bull Durham tag setting from my blouse pocket and he hollered down, 'Hey Red! How approximately rolling me a cigarette?' So I did, and we began out speakme, and proper off we appeared to strike some kind of rapport. That became the begin of a friendship that lasted till Borglum died. We had u.S.A.And downs, but we were typically buddies. He modified into a undergo to get along element sometimes, and temperamental due to the fact the very satan, however beneath all of it he become in reality a tremendous guy and a first rate man. I always respectable him, and I think he usually respectable me."

Not considerably, the most tedious part of the challenge come to be carving the finer factors of the faces. According to Nick Clifford, "This is what they referred to as honeycombing. This grow to be the subsequent to the very last step of completing the faces. And they may drill those holes in. The pointers or Mr. Borglum might tell them how deep to drill the holes. You can see they have been setting out more rock down proper proper right here than they have been up right right here. And it end up probably right close to the face, likely it emerge as on like on a cheek or a few element like that. And they may take a sharp pointed piece of steel and they'd hit in every this sort of holes. Eventually this rock would possibly pop off, after which they'll use a bumping hammer -- they called it bumping -- and that would smooth the rock up similar to it's far in recent times, which you see it on the mountain."

A photograph of labor being performed on Mount Rushmore

This manner became to begin with made even extra difficult via the horrible tool the men have been compelled to use. The drill-bits, produced on net web page with the beneficial resource of a nearby blacksmith, fast dulled with non-stop use, but no person need to persuade him to supply any better bits till a touch old-fashioned competition came into play. One man later described, "A salesman for screw-bits confirmed up at the mountain. A screw-bit could drill approximately seven feet earlier than getting silly, in contrast to about feet with the strong drills we were the usage of. Of direction, the screw-bits had been more pricey because on the same time as you dulled one you changed it with a brand new one, whilst those we had been using is probably sharpened time and again over again. Well, Borglum stated he modified into going to buy 'em anyways, and if he had it'd of placed the blacksmith out of a interest. When the blacksmith saw that hand-writing on the wall he requested for one extra chance, and Borglum gave it to him. After that you definitely couldn't put on absolutely considered one of his bits out!"

Of route, coping with silly drills turn out to be far from the most disturbing element about walking at the challenge. Most of the men recommended testimonies for the rest of their lives about what it become need to keep off the factor of stable granite greater than forty recollections inside the air jogging on Washington's brow. Red Anderson advised a specially harrowing story approximately while the character above him set free an excessive amount of slack at the same time as he modified into struggling to launch a specially recalcitrant tool anchor: "I just flipped backward right out into place. I fell loose for about twenty-5 toes, then I hit the surrender of the slack. The jerk darn near snapped me in ! Then I slammed into the face of the cliff and sincerely type of bounced to and fro in the direction of it. Somehow I'd had experience enough to fold my hands in the front of my face once I started out falling. My fingers and hands have been given skinned up pretty terrible, but if I hadn't completed that the Lord simplest knows what sort of a face I'd be wearing now. And I can let you know this: If you fall off a cliff and anticipate to be supported with the aid of the usage of a cable that isn't there it'll surprise you some."

The longer the men labored together, the nearer they have end up to every different, positive together through manner of a mixture of shared threat and accomplishment. They additionally developed a few interesting strategies to "welcome" new individuals to their elite group. One worker described how new humans have been initiated: "You'd take keep of his cable in which it ran over the rock on pinnacle, and if you went at it actual sluggish you could really gradually increase him up a foot or so without him knowin' he'd ever been lifted. Then you'd permit skip of the cable and of path he'd drop with a helluva jerk, and, why, it'd simply scare the waddin' out of him.

Chapter 6: Double Whammy

"They had this nearly double whammy. The entire u . S . A ., in reality lots of the area changed into wrapped up in this horrendous economic melancholy. Then on top of that have become the Dust Bowl days. There come to be no rain; the farmers need to boom no plant life. What little they may decorate, it grow to be nearly now not feasible to market. They had been leaving the state in droves. Those who stayed pressured why they have been still right here. And in 1932, the art work at Rushmore had floor to a complete halt. And all over again there has been the threat of this complete element honestly in no way being completed." - Dr. Karl Wegner, Peter Norbeck's grandson

July 4th, 1930 located the primary critical "show" in the Mount Rushmore undertaking as Washington's face modified into unveiled for journalists from around the u . S .. This stirred up all the exposure that Borglum was hoping to advantage, and within the yr that located, extra than 27,000 humans traveled to the region to appearance what he referred to as "The Shrine of Democracy."

This interest proved to be a shot in the arm to every the planners and that guys running on the challenge. Glowing with pleasure, Borglum publicly anticipated that the entire undertaking is probably completed via the surrender of 1934, however he may additionally want to fast be showed wrong. To make matters worse, Senator Norbeck, who had the type of knack for securing authorities investment, become diagnosed with cancer and had to spend a whole lot of his time with medical docs in choice to Congressmen.

On top of those troubles, the mountain itself appeared to expose on them. John Houser defined, "They were aware about route that there had been going to be, faults and cracks in the rock, a number of them had been hard to discover. In fact they started out Jefferson off to Washington's proper, and they determined available wasn't sufficient stone there. The stone have come to be too crumbly and it simply wasn't of suitable first-class." Robin Carter delivered, "They had to blast that off after 18 months of exertions, which should were coronary coronary heart breaking to try this, as tight as cash modified into, and then to blast off what they had spent all that point doing … He did now not display any depression, even to Mary very a bargain. One letter that I positioned in which he come to be in Washington for months in search of to get money for Rushmore and it grow to be a horrible time and he wrote to her and said, 'I'm just ill approximately what's going on, however this is the time to be courageous.' And you understand I assume his spirit just stored him going and Mary stored him going."

Indeed, Borglum remained determined, plunging earlier whilst the Rushmore Association persevered to feature within the crimson. Mary Vhay recalled, "My father by no means preferred to confess any form of failure, and certainly he did not need to admit it. I'm positive he did with mom, but he did not with us. I suggest it became commonly going to be, everything have emerge as going to be all proper ... I don't anticipate he would were able to hold on if it hadn't been for my mother. She became continuously there, now not riding him, but building up his ego, making him conscious that he come to be a superb sculptor ... He corresponded with all people you can consider. And I imply from the heads of u . S . A . On all of the way right down to the almost the garbage men. Probably no longer the rubbish men because of the reality he probably hadn't paid them."

Paying human beings become regularly some element Borglum felt become beneath his dignity. While he may need to make certain those working for him at the mountain had been compensated for their efforts, he could not apprehend why all people else may need his coins. Bob Hayes knowledgeable a tale he heard from his father, one in every of Borglum's personnel: "He become discovering the nation and he stopped at a touch station and he desired to refill his automobile. And the younger station attendant, you realise, stated, 'Well you recognize I need to have coins first.' He stated 'Well do no longer you understand who I am?' And the attendant stated, 'I realise precisely who you're. That's why I must have the coins first.' That unique operator later admitted, "I in no way had been given any of Borglum's enterprise employer after that, however that became all right with me. The station guys who did promote him gas said it changed into normally a losing proposition." When absolutely everyone at a loss for words his "divine proper," Borglum was quick to reply: "Don't those crazy humans recognize what I'm doing for them? Just because of the fact I actually have an unpaid grocery bill at Hermosa, they're calling me a deadbeat! My God! I'm giving them a few thing an amazing way to carry a thousand million greenbacks into the ones hills, and that they carp at me due to the fact I haven't paid for a piddling parcel of groceries!"

In fact, Borglum's experience of his non-public significance extended to his dating with Congressional leaders as properly. Wagner cited, "Borglum had this tendency to reveal up in Washington unannounced and appear in advance than committees and try and time desk appointments with the president. He might possibly supply one set of monetary projections to as a minimum one committee or to at the least one senator or to 1 congressman, and inner a consider of hours or days come up with every other set of figures, or he ought to mention he ought to finish this undertaking for $250,000, while anyone sitting within the room knew that there has been no manner in which that entire mission can be finished for $250,000."

Houser agreed, which include, "A amount of times my father and Borglum have been in the Senate searching out investment for Mount Rushmore. So one time they have been up in the balcony at the Senate, and the Bill turn out to be at the floor and one of the Senators stood up and he modified into raging in opposition to

Borglum, and he have become calling, 'Why are we looking to appropriate price range for this loopy genius?' And then that brought on Borglum. Borglum jumped to his feet, but in advance than he may additionally need to say a few component my dad grabbed him thru way of the coattails and pulled him down, and he stated, 'He referred to as you a genius did now not he?'"

Ultimately, Norbeck had to take Borglum to challenge for his arrogance: "Isn't the fact that all future time will view this artwork as Borglum's paintings enough unto you? Why now not permit the men who do little things get credit score score for their little things? ... Big guys need to ... be content material fabric cloth with the very last vindication in choice to looking for to hog all of it. Isn't it enough to be known as the arena's best sculptor with out furthermore yearning the handclapping of folks that stay inside the styx [sic] and don't recognize what it is all approximately?"

Chapter 7: Heated Arguments and Conflicts

Picture of employees on Mount Rushmore

"Grandpa Norbeck have become the only individual whom Borglum reliable enough to simply accept his judgment and surrender approximately topics. And in a number of his heated arguments and conflicts with Boland specifically, however in no manner restricted to John Boland, Grandpa Norbeck turn out to be able to step in and remedy or at the least in part remedy a number of the conflicts. And then a few trouble ought to erupt all all all over again." - Dr. Karl Wegner

Ironically, the monetary catastrophe that almost derailed the Mount Rushmore assignment subsequently have end up its salvation. In 1932, President Herbert Hoover began out to location into vicinity some public applications designed to offer unemployed Americans a threat to make cash, and Norbeck controlled to get $a hundred,000 of the coins earmarked for his domestic canine mission. He additionally persuaded the nascent National Parks Service to create a extremely-current national park round Mount Rushmore. Still benefitting from the reputation left to it via its founder, Theodore Roosevelt, the NPS turn out to be capable of funnel even more money into the monument.

Throughout all of the modifications, Borglum became capable of hold the loyalty of most of his personnel, no matter the fact that, as one placed it, he emerge as "a heckuva stone-carver, however he ain't no sweet-talker." Though they did not normally understand his innovative temperament, they normally reputable him as someone who modified into determined to do a extremely good pastime, even if he made lawsuits. One worker defined one such criticism: "I'm not happy with the manner it turns underneath there and is derived in the direction of the collar. You circulate on down there Payne. I need those points very carefully examined. I'll be down there in a couple of minutes." Vhay moreover described her father's manipulate fashion: "Dad ought to probably get livid at them inside the event that they were silly, 'reason he could not stand stupidity. Anybody have to make a mistake once, however not or 3 times, and within the occasion that they did or 3 instances he might also need to generally have them fired. And that come to be some different undertaking that Lincoln had due to the fact if it changed into an splendid guy Lincoln may also have to speak him into coming decrease returned over again. And then Dad would be shape of amazed to look him and he then he'd say 'What have you ever been doing, Lincoln?'"

Lincoln grow to be Borglum's 21 12 months antique son, who have been added onto the mission. Accustomed to his father's moods and wishes, he furthermore had his mom's way with people and therefore made an brilliant pass-among. According to at least one worker, "He grew up with the mountain. Working so near with his father, it surely had to be catchy. I suggest he had a vision furthermore of what the mountain have end up going to be like. You might probably in no way see him sittin' down. If you may look up why Lincoln could be up on pinnacle searching down or lookin' on the faces, or in which the guys had been carving. He turn out to be everywhere within the mountain. You in no way saw him get mad or to chunk every person out. You have to chuckle with Lincoln and feature a exceptional time. When we went on our baseball journeys Lincoln should generally move, and if we did some issue unique, why, he'd pat us at the decrease back and inform us what a notable hobby we might finished. And he changed into most effective a tremendous guy."

Lincoln and his father

Lincoln joined the Mount Rushmore organization sincerely as Borglum come to be starting artwork on the second president, Thomas Jefferson, and the timing couldn't have been better for the reason that Jefferson proved to be the most important challenge of they all. When the guys made the primary few blasts into the part of the mountain set aside for his likeness, they had been disenchanted to discover now not difficult granite but smooth feldspar, which they needed to cast off from the president's lip and update with an amalgamation of lead, linseed oil and granite dust. This modified into a tedious and time-ingesting enterprise, no longer to mention luxurious.

Thanks to the latest property of funding, via the middle of 1933, work have grow to be over again being finished at the mountain, however with extra cash came extra tips. For one trouble, the NPS had appointed John Boland of Rapid City to supervise the investment of the challenge, which intended Borglum needed to go to him on every occasion he favored get proper of access to to greater price variety. A businessman himself, Boland have become aware about preserving a sharp eye on the bottom line and become committed to handling the usa's cash as if it became his very private. Not fairly, this indignant Borglum, who as quickly as wrote, "I've were given to visit Rapid City, and punch a nice son of a bitch proper in the nostril." On a few exclusive event, while Boland refused to authorize fee for a few exposure photos Borglum had ordered, Borglum wrote to him in a rage, "I have nowadays obtained a photostat of your letter to D'Emery discrediting my order.... In the Stone Mountain artwork I felt it essential to govern the publicity ... I act at the equal conditions for the Mount Rushmore Commission ... [which] had resulted inside the most inexperienced exposure in artwork in cutting-edge instances ... Interference with it is incomprehensible ... the query of matching and so securing a similarly thousand does no longer excuse the impropriety nor wisdome [sic] of your interference ... The exposure I even have secured for South Dakota is paintings [sic] masses of masses — and yet you, as an professional of the State and Commission, restriction me in those processes!!"

In addition to steady stresses over coins, there was additionally a developing experience in Borglum's heart that his authority have become being undermined on the aspect of the mountain. To a excellent amount, this modified into right, even though this end up now not normally a awful issue because it were given the paintings executed. For instance, even as he located out that Bill Tallman, his superintendent of operations for the beyond 4 years, have become selecting and deciding on what orders he concept had to be obeyed with the aid of the use of himself and others, Borglum wrote to Boland, "I demand that my officials or guys aren't demorailized [sic] nor corrupted thru telling them they want no longer obey my orders, or telling them a few factor the least bit that pertains to my art work. I am accountable for Billy's behavior— I am responsible for his artwork, I shall push aside him if he disobeys me. He is broken hearted over the twin characteristic you've got pressured him to play.... The Sculptor on my own selects and determines who, while, wherein, and the way, the class of fellows and company from the men hired, He is in entire fee of layout, control, and course of the paintings and interference with the guys for political or splendid reasons will no longer be accepted."

Norbeck, combating for his lifestyles, have emerge as too exhausted to address Borglum and in the long run wrote to him, "Your letter report will get us all in problem ... If Congress should decide to analyze, it might finish that the Commission is made from a gaggle of crooks, or that the artist is a nut— or each." But subtlety come to be vain on each person as pushed as Borglum have become, which forced Norbeck to ultimately write to the sculptor, "I actually have in no way diagnosed Mr. Boland to do a dishonorable detail ... If [he] is doing the belongings you say he is, it's miles a rely of proof. If it's miles proper, the problem have to be laid earlier than the Board ... I even have presently come to sense that you can do something so you can prevent the very last touch of Rushmore. I might not be amazed any morning to discover a declaration within the papers that Rushmore has end up now not viable due to interference from politicians. The public will revel in the type of assertion from you. You will experience the public's response in your statement. You may be sitting pretty for some time … despite the fact that this sort of declaration is without foundation … after the climax of this remember comes, I do no longer know a manner to select out up the quantities … I informed you within the preceding letter that if I modified into now not capable of result in harmonious paintings the various Sculptor and the Commission I would no longer stay on the Commission … There isn't always any non-public unwell will on my issue…. I receive the explanation that you were unwell, but you're simply in a disturbed body of thoughts which does now not bode well for the progress of the artwork. I actually have remodeled seven years of attempt in this art work. It has been a heavy drain on my energy and handbag. It continues getting worse."

By 1935, Norbeck knew that his time have come to be walking out. Summoning his ultimate little little little bit of power, he made a totally closing trip to Washington to make his very last appeal to Congress. Looking at their gaunt and suffering colleague, the Senate short agreed to pour some different $ hundred,000 of federal coins into the mission. Not long afterwards, Norbeck wrote, "A week as soon as I am long long gone, they may start to forget about approximately me. A decade and most people of South Dakota might be not able to even consider my call." Fortunately, Norbeck have become mounted incorrect, as one South Dakotan historian nowadays said, "Anyone who is aware about our kingdom's facts might virtually rank Peter Norbeck as our maximum interesting and brilliant person. He come to be a completely modern Republican governor and U.S. Senator who did more to form our records than all the relaxation of our governors mixed."

Chapter 8: A Shrine to Democracy

"I want you, Mr. President, to devote this memorial as a Shrine to Democracy; to name upon the people of the earth for a hundred thousand future years to take a look at the perception and to look what manner of fellows struggled proper here to installation self-decided government inside the western international. With the prayer that it shall no longer perish from the earth." – Borglum's creation of President Franklin Roosevelt

In 1936, Franklin Roosevelt got here to South Dakota to dedicate the completed Jefferson. He began his speech by way of saying, "I anticipate, my friends, that there are individuals who knowledgeable me approximately this in the early days – really one in every of them have come to be Mr.

Borglum and the alternative have become Senator Norbeck. On many activities, while a modern undertaking is provided to you on paper after which, in a while, you notice the accomplishment, you are disillusioned: but it is simply the opposite of that during what we're searching at now. I had visible the pix: I had visible the drawings and I had talked with folks that are responsible for this extremely good art work, and yet I had had no concept until approximately ten mins in the past now not first-rate of its charge but of its everlasting beauty and of its everlasting significance. Mr. Borglum has well stated that this will be a monument and an idea for the continuance of the democratic-republican shape of government, no longer handiest in our private loved u .

S . A ., however, we are hoping, at some stage in the world. This is the second one determination. There may be others via distinct presidents in particular years. When we get thru, there may be some factor for the American people that allows you to final through not truly generations however for heaps and masses of years, and I think that we will in all likelihood meditate a touch on the ones Americans 10000 years from now whilst the weathering on the face of Washington and Jefferson and Lincoln shall have proceeded to perhaps a depth of a tenth of an inch – meditate and wonder what our descendants, and I anticipate they may however be right right here, will recollect us. Let us preference that at the least they may deliver us the advantage of the doubt –

that they will be given as proper with we have were given really striven every day and technology to keep for our descendants a top notch land to stay in and a decent form of presidency to perform below."

Norbeck barely lived to be at the dedication, death only a few months later. However, Wegner later admitted, "It have become one of the first rate days of my grandfather's existence. I anticipate for him, I, as a minimum I simply have questioned if it didn't turn out to be a touch like that of Borglum, that this changed into one of the crowning accomplishments of his lifestyles, to have made this possible. As my grandfather had said that Mount Rushmore isn't always a shaggy dog story, it isn't a dream. It's actual. It's there."

Much to the marvel of many, the paintings on the project persevered even after Norbeck's lack of life. Ironically, with out someone to placate him, Borglum matured to the factor that he can also need to calm himself or maybe work higher with others. Nick Clifford conceded, "Mr. Borglum always complained that the humans him whilst he become doing his paintings but he ought to continuously save you while someone desired to invite a query or some element like that. He'd need to prevent and talk to the human beings too, so he must supply an reason behind what he modified into undertaking. He used to inform people, 'The faces are in the mountain. All I must do is deliver them out.'"

Robin Carter agreed, announcing her grandfather "in no manner gave up seeing it as amazing artwork. And lots of humans might argue with that, that it have become extra of an engineering undertaking than some thing else, however he in fact noticed it as art -- that he have become going to hold the existence of those 4 human beings to the principle part, definitely as you would if you had been doing a small statue of them."

It should no longer be tough to don't forget that someone as temperamental and volatile as Borglum may begin to lose interest in the task by the time he modified into midway via, but the contrary changed into the case. During the overdue Thirties, whilst operating on Lincoln and Roosevelt, Borglum wrote, "Have to climb down over the face of Washington and decrease returned up the face of Jefferson. I want to be getting tired of it all, however I am no longer . . . I now see that I can be able to make a real art work of paintings of this huge group. Back in my coronary coronary heart that has been a doubt for decades. I in truth don't have any help in that; in that I am simply on my own."

Such feedback were widespread of Borglum, who preferred to appearance himself as a voice crying in the desert on behalf of his terrible, disregarded venture, however in fact, he nonetheless had many humans assisting his efforts. Moreover, for every imaginative and prescient he conceived, there have been a dozen or extra men who needed to go up on the mountain and make it a truth. As Carter positioned it, "Gutzon seems to have complained loads about the unskilled personnel that he changed into faced with, but truely he grow to be very glad with the guys and clearly pleased with the reality that he'd been capable of train those humans who've been miners and who have been just neighborhood, who had in no way labored on a mountain in advance than, did no longer recognize some thing about art work and he'd been capable of take them and train them into doing what he favored finished."

In truth, Borglum bear in mind to preserve the challenge for years, announcing at a few degree within the 1937 self-control of Abraham Lincoln, "Where greatness is promised, history and civilization will in no way forgive its absence or the ones accountable for its failure ... This monument has however a unmarried reason, to borrow a line from Lincoln's Gettysburg speech: 'That those guys shall now not have lived in useless; that under God the kingdom they built shall have a latest transport of freedom, and that a government of the humans, via manner of the people, and for the humans shall now not perish from the earth!'"

Pictures of employees on Lincoln's likeness

Unfortunately, Borglum persevered to get in his non-public way, at the whole because of his personal tactlessness. For example, in May 1938, the subsequent story made its manner at some point of the united states of a and all the manner to Washington, D.C.: "Gutzon Borglum, sculptor, blamed community politics, the previous day, for slowing artwork on the Mount

Rushmore countrywide memorial ... 'I clearly have have been given to have greater guys and extra electricity,' Borglum informed the residence library committee inside the direction of the discussions on the Keller invoice to create a modern-day day Mount Rushmore memorial fee ... 'I can't surrender the heads with those miners. I sincerely have have been given to have carvers and that they block me every time,' Borglum protested in charging the engineer for the prevailing ... fee ... 'interferes with the jobs.' Borglum contended neighborhood hobbies dictated who need to be hired to help him. In this he end up supported by the use of Representative Keller (D-Ill.), committee chairman, who said, 'sure, John Boland of Rapid City runs the whole thing.'"

Accustomed to Borglum's conduct, Boland wasted no time responding. He wrote the following to the Associated Press: "Since I virtually have grow to be a member of the Commission in March, 1929, there has been no political interference Nationally, State or county, each on the part of the Republican or Democratic businesses. On the opposite, every political activities … have been maximum beneficial. The Commission has in no manner been financially capable of offer extra energy. To provide greater strength as suggested would possibly imply almost all finances would probably ought to be expended for present day system and little cash is probably left to hold at the paintings. To my knowledge, no former superintendent, nor the existing resident engineer has dictated who have to be employed … nor have I attempted to manipulate employment of the men. Mr. Borglum has constantly directed who need to be employed … via the superintendents and his assistant, his son Lincoln. I definitely have in no way interfered with Mr. Borglum in his artwork. I actually have endeavored to conduct satisfactory the sincerely commercial enterprise affairs of the Commission … in a businesslike manner. Mr. Borglum is an artist and I am a businessman. Therefore it's far simplest herbal that we have to at times disagree concerning the company capabilities of the Commission. Such differences, but, have in no manner been immoderate and an amicable knowledge has generally been reached. My best desire is to have the Mount

Rushmore project finished within the brilliant viable manner, and to have Mr. Borglum hold on his outstanding work, with the in a characteristic help of his son, Lincoln, the ongoing cooperation of the Commission, and the efficient supervision of the National Park Service."

Nonetheless, through 1940, Borglum had emerge as one of the maximum famous artists in America, and his massive task stuck the hearts and imaginations of people at some point of the country. Therefore, he had a positive quantity of political clout and acquired this particular round, with the Commission being disbanded and more manage positioned in his private hands. However, regardless of this freedom, he turn out to be not capable of make tremendous development and soon discovered himself decrease lower back beneath the authority of some other rate. He located this specially grievous, for the reason that new fee forced him to prevent paintings on his treasured "Hall," a garage room carved into the granite. He described, "I want, someplace in America, on or near the Rockies, the spine of the Continent, thus far removed from succeeding, egocentric, coveting civilizations, a few ft of stone that bears witness, incorporates the likeness, the dates, a phrase or two of the remarkable subjects we completed as a Nation, placed so high it can not pay to drag them down for lesser abilties. Hence, allow us to area there, carved high, as near heaven as we're able to, the terms of our leaders, their faces, to expose posterity what manner of fellows they were. Then breathe a prayer that those facts will endure till the wind and rain on my own shall located on them away."

Borglum had correct reason to be worried on the time, because the entire u . S . A . Have come to be watching Nazi Germany run roughshod throughout Europe. Preparing for the battle that it appeared might inevitably obtain America, Congress felt it is able to not keep to spend taxpayer coins on an art work project, regardless of how big and well-known it is probably.

Sadly, simply months after Congress refused to fund anymore art work, Borglum died from complications after a cutting-edge surgical treatment. Wegner later determined, "Lincoln Borglum, of route, had taken over after his father died. By then a prime a part of the paintings had been completed, but there has been despite the fact that a honest amount of trimming and cleansing as much as do across the faces and, and the collars of and shoulders of some of the figures. And the exceptional hall of statistics that have been every other splendid ambition and dream of Borglum's quite an lousy lot perished in the method. The paintings at Rushmore virtually kind of step by step drew to a close."

According to Lincoln Borglum, speaking at that time, "The sculpture artwork at the faces come to be completed earlier than Father's death, and the skills of the 4 presidents will not be touched. We've have been given to finish the hair on Jefferson, Roosevelt, and Lincoln and do some art work on

Lincoln's collar and on his head. That's the immediately software program."

The final paintings turn out to be finished on October 31, 1941, just 5 weeks earlier than he Japanese bombed Pearl Harbor. By then, 14 years and almost one million bucks have been spent on the most important monument on within the international, but within the 80 five years for the purpose that undertaking become commenced, greater than 50 million people from all over the global have visited it. As Nick Clifford positioned it, "I appearance up on the mountain and I consider Mr. Borglum, what a first rate guy he changed into, what a extraordinary sculptor he have emerge as. I recollect Lincoln, who became a chum to all of the men. And then I recall all the guys that I worked with and knew, and the manner committed those guys have been to the mountain, and they're all lengthy beyond now. And I ought to prevent now."

Chapter 9: The Creation of Rushmore

Originally only a rustic project supposed for the viewing of residents of South Dakota and its surrounding states, Mount Rushmore have become a rustic huge paintings of artwork. It have become first estimated in the early Nineteen Twenties via manner of a rustic historian named Doane Robinson who desired to growth tourism in South Dakota, after he'd heard of plans to carve exceptional distinguished leaders of the Confederacy into Georgia's Stone Mountain. Robinson then commissioned the talents of Gutzon Borglum, an American sculptor who changed into definitely dwelling in Europe at that point.

Borglum desired the concept, and agreed to visit the Black Hills of South Dakota as quickly as he may also additionally need to that allows you to assist Robinson pick out out a mountain. Where Robinson had favored to chisel the faces of heroes from the Wild West, Borglum advised instead that they choose four beloved American presidents. George Washington, Thomas Jefferson, and Abraham Lincoln came truely, but many humans were pressured with the aid of Borglum's insistence that Theodore Roosevelt be the fourth. After receiving Congress' popularity of funding, Borglum employed loads of human beings and spent the subsequent 14 years completing the undertaking that might in the end value the usa a total of $989,992.32.

Gutzon Borglum's dad and mom were spiritual Mormons who moved from Denmark to Utah within the 1850s. But at that factor, Utah country authorities had in recent times began cracking down at the Mormon marital traditions of polygamy, and so the Borglums moved to Idaho, wherein Gutzon turn out to be born in 1867. After finishing his number one education, Gutzon Borglum graduated from scientific university and started out his first practice in Fremont, Nebraska.

Borglum determined his vintage flame, however, to be inside the arts, and so he decided to move to New York to examine portray. There, he met his spouse, who changed into additionally his teacher, and they moved to Paris, France to have a have a examine together below properly-set up and renown painters and sculptors. In 1909, Borglum and his spouse once more to New York in which they opened a studio displaying Borglum's artwork. One of his portions, an large marble bust of Abraham Lincoln, earned Borglum public attention whilst President Roosevelt requested that the sculpture be displayed on the White House for the duration of the centennial celebration of Lincoln's starting.

From the developing recognition that Roosevelt's popularity gave Borglum, the United Daughters of the Confederacy commissioned him to create a large commemoration out of Georgia's Stone Mountain in 1915. While this number one enjoy in taking over a large-scale sculpture in the end proved to be a whole failure, it no matter the reality that gave Borglum the very experience with explosives, jackhammers, and unique strategies of carving massive figures that led Doane Robinson to are searching for for his abilties for what may grow to be Mount Rushmore.

A usa historian and renowned poet, Robinson desired to commemorate the records of United States growth, the accomplishments of its pioneers, and maintain the overall nostalgia that had come to be related to the brilliant American West. To reap this, he expected the faces of well-known Wild West heroes carved into the thing of a mountain; e.G., Meriwether Lewis and William Clark, General George Armstrong Custer, Jedidiah Smith, or maybe Native Americans like Red Cloud and Sacajawea.

In August of 1925, Borglum traveled to South Dakota's Custer State Park to choose out the mountain that turned into high-quality perfect for the assignment. Although precise mountains had been taller and wider than Mount Rushmore, Borglum decided on the height for its massive granite and the reality that it become crafted from 4 best crevices deep enough to offer the superb angular complexity he had hoped for.

However, this mission couldn't be commissioned sincerely for the sake of artwork, however furthermore to attract sightseers to South Dakota and stimulate the u . S .'s financial gadget through a few issue tourism the monument might appeal to. And on that take a look at, Borglum understood what might deliver inside the variety of travelers Robinson grow to be aiming for. Carving United States presidents may make the memorial a rustic wide birthday party instead of a surely a close-by one. In the telegram he despatched to Robinson in 1924, Borglum wrote as regards to carving the faces of Washington and Lincoln, "Let us hold to that unbeatable and inspiring concept of those lone giants, popularity on top of America, George cloaked and Abe hatless, their figures growing out of the mother ledge. That can be enough."

Robinson agreed completely with Borglum's assessment and granted him complete modern autonomy as he knew the enterprise have to superb gain public beneficial aid if it appealed to severa business interests. In an interview with Specialty Salesman Magazine, Borglum is quoted as announcing, "I found out that the not unusual person in South Dakota, whilst he become approached in regard to financing Mount Rushmore Memorial, should think of it in phrases of bucks and cents.... We tried to speak to the humans of that kingdom in only the ones terms."

Nevertheless, no matter the fact that the 2 innovative visionaries of Mount Rushmore agreed that the challenge's achievement trusted their functionality to draw on commercial dreams, they however felt annoying about the problem as they worried it may bring about unbecoming interpretations regarding the monument's motivation and significance.

In 1924, Borglum and Robinson made the choice that the number one of the 4 presidents is probably Washington and

Lincoln. Borglum proposed Jefferson as the following face, and an apparent one for the reason that he had not only been the writer of the us' true Declaration of Independence, however become additionally responsible for securing the Louisiana territory. It is not any twist of fate that thru the Purchase, the U.S. Received the very Black Hills which Mount Rushmore emerge as a part of.

After identifying upon Jefferson, Borglum suggested Theodore Roosevelt due to the truth the fourth and final portrayal. Out of the 4 of Borglum's options, it changed into best Roosevelt that produced any questions and disagreements. Even Robinson criticized the idea as he felt that Roosevelt became not nearly as esteemed as Washington, Lincoln, and/or Jefferson.

Although Borglum never expounded upon why it have become he selected Roosevelt, most historians agree that he most in all likelihood felt indebted to the president as it become Roosevelt who became responsible for Borglum's countrywide reputation as a tremendous artist.

After the pix had been determined on, Borglum provided the thoughts to the Mount Rushmore Association's government committee. As if the big task would possibly now not be hard sufficient, Borglum have come to be faced with the mission of sculpting Mount Rushmore for the duration of the Great Depression. The committee permitted the assignment's plans and agreed to finance it via way of supplying the lofty sum of $four hundred,000, however Borglum knew that range must nice cowl superb preliminary costs together with the advent of plaster moldings, and the infrastructures for rope-and-pulley lifts that were to be utilized by workers, systems upon which they might paintings, and bunkhouses wherein they could live during the duration of the task.

Luckily for Borglum, phrase emerge as spreading that President Coolidge have been actively considering spending his subsequent holiday out west. Recognizing that this sort of visit could be an opportunity you obtain extra funding, Borglum met with South Dakota governor William Bulow to persuade him to ask the President to the Black Hills. Shortly after, Senator Peter Norbeck delivered the invitation in person to Coolidge, who then preferred it and planned his journey there that changed into to begin on June 16, 1927.

Word spread short at some point of South Dakota, and Governor Bulow felt an increasing number of strain as the general public's delight and anticipation escalated. Tasked with the massive duty of precise the President of the us, Bulow planned a rodeo in his honor, a party hosted thru the Sioux, and horseback using training.

However, the president changed into making plans to stay for 3 complete weeks, and so Bulow may want to want many more thoughts and sports activities than that. He then determined that a trout fishing tour might possibly possibly be the first-rate manner to occupy the president's time. To make certain that it grow to be a a success experience for him, Bulow ordered hundreds of growing older trout, lethargic fish which have been fats and gradual, to be dumped in the streams wherein Coolidge have emerge as to fish.

It took a excellent deal less than ten minutes for Coolidge to entice five sizeable trout, and the following morning he invited Bulow over for breakfast wherein they feasted at the president's successful capture. Falling in love with the Black Hills, Coolidge extended his tour and stayed within the region for numerous months. The fulfillment of this journey made the president a passionate backer of Mount Rushmore.

Coolidge pledged his assist, and due to this, Senator Norbeck organized his request for Washington D.C. Looking for $500,000 of congressional funding. He sent Borglum to petition the secretary, and awkwardly, Borglum mistakenly requested for simply $250,000, assuring Congress that he may additionally need you bought private investment for the alternative half of of the sum.

Upon coming across Borglum's blunder, Norbeck have become reportedly flabbergasted as he have been confident that Congress should cowl the entire charge based totally absolutely mostly on how excited and approving President Coolidge had been of the assignment. There changed into, but, now not whatever more he also can want to do. The appropriation exceeded quick via both the House and the Senate, and President Coolidge made the invoice valid through signing it on February 25, 1929.

Chapter 10: Patriotism and Commercialism

"It is pretty out of location inside the wilds of the Black Hills, in which God's statuary surpasses any possible concept of mere man."

J.B. Townsley

While many citizens of South Dakota and its Black Hills had been excited at the possibility of a grand countrywide monument being constructed of their home usa, Mount Rushmore's creators predicted that they could continually even though want to face some critics. They started out to strategize beforehand of time, and the number one way wherein they went about this modified into to emphasize the carving's patriotic significance. Borglum knew that converting the heroes of the Wild West with the images of reputable American presidents turn out to be a totally realistic concept.

Still, Robinson and Borglum understood that totally relying on the Mount Rushmore mission's patriotic appeal need to nonetheless no longer be enough to advantage the assist and funding that they nevertheless wished. Not excellent have grow to be the task pricey and stressful years of labor, but the creators additionally faced folks that outright rejected it altogether. Due to the truth that they could want to use explosives, many residents of the Black Hills appeared it as an utter desecration towards the Divine's natural introduction that modified into the mountain itself.

In a letter written to Robinson, Maude Hoover stated, "Why have to we add to, or alternatively, desecrate, the art work of nature with the puny artwork of man? What if we do have a amazing cliff face 'with now not whatever on it' amongst those towering peaks?... Please Mr. Robinson, do not use your have an impact on in competition to us Black Hillers on this recollect. We love our Black Hills with a love that grows with acquaintance. Leave them to us as nature left them, deep, quiet, majestic, natural."

Other letters poured in, too. The Dakota Republican's editor, J.B. Townsley wrote, "It is substantially out of vicinity in the wilds of the Black Hills, wherein God's statuary surpasses any possible concept of mere man."

Nevertheless, Robinson could not be deterred quite so effortlessly. Criticizing Mount Rushmore challengers, he hired his very very own non secular rhetoric even as he asserted that, "God most effective makes a Michelangelo or a Gutzon Borglum as quickly as in one thousand years." Responding to the developing sentiment that the venture may be an absolute desecration, Robinson countered, "Of course God made the Needles [which was originally intended to be the project's location] as he made the whole lot else that guy has taken to himself and improved and beautified. That is what God made guys and things for. There isn't any properly judgment I am positive in the desecration idea."

Robinson changed into no longer, however, truely debating as even though he have been some kind of felony expert who did no longer really agree with his very private arguments. In reality, Robinson have become identified for having an prolonged facts of regarding nature's creative and scientific renovations because the achievement of divine duties that he taken into consideration to be basically religious.

In any other letter he had written in 1925, Robinson wrote, "God did no longer pretty entire his hobby inside the Harney district [the Hills south of Rushmore], however left it for man to return returned into that segment and create Sylvan Lake, the very jewel of the phase. God typically leaves it to guy to finish his art work-it really is why we have were given Burbanks and Hansens growing the seed of beauty which God planted."

Although effective and convincing, the Rushmore creators had to assert more arguments to justify the venture than genuinely Robinson's spiritual claims. Both guys agreed that it is probably vital to connect the carving's patriotic sentiments with the monetary; i.E., the increase in tourism the monument should deliver to South Dakota and its subsequently promising worthwhile ability.

Borglum seized every chance furnished to him to boast the significant business possibilities that Mount Rushmore could create. In one interview, Borglum stated, "I placed out that the commonplace person in South Dakota, whilst he modified into approached in regard to financing Mount Rushmore Memorial, may additionally need to take into account it in phrases of greenbacks and cents.... We attempted to talk to the human beings of that nation in only those phrases."

Borglum was so a success that Specialty Salesman Magazine said his abilties and declared Borglum to be one of the most "super income guys of America." The magazine's writer wrote, "Borglum did no longer stay at the rate of fantastic art work in making the lives of the men and women who observed the excellent figures... More livable... Instead he compiled figures showing an estimate of the wide variety of folks that is probably anticipated to visit South Dakota because of the Memorial." Despite Borglum and Robinson's willingness to publically rent the challenge's business incentive, in non-public they worried that this kind of tactic ought to possibly lead some people to make distorted and unsavory interpretations of the monument.

In a non-public letter written to Robinson, Borglum expressed non-public convictions and that his private innovative integrity had been causing him to struggle with the financial advertising and marketing campaign. "Not a tenth of 1 percentage of the masses who come lengthy distances to see this artwork-especially because of the reality it is large-make a contribution a unmarried profound idea on each the attempt to bring together the soul and individual of fellows in such dimensions, or do they see an entire lot beyond the scale, and very little, if in any respect, of why it became performed."

However, Borglum and Robinson have been now not the great human beings concerned with the venture to have felt alternatively sickly approximately linking paintings and patriotic motivation with commercial hobbies. Many of their fellow Rushmore proponents struggled with the advertising marketing campaign as nicely, or even went up to now as to name it sacrilegious.

For example, the whiskey logo, Seagram's, attempted to launch a broadcast business with an photograph that featured 3 of the carving's presidents—Washington, Jefferson, and Lincoln—sitting around eating, and underneath the depiction observe the phrases, "George went out to get every different 5th." Absolutely mortified via the use of the ad, the Mount Rushmore National Monument Society end up able to have it pulled earlier than Seagram's must distribute it.

Nevertheless, the economic advertising marketing campaign for Rushmore end up so powerful that particular companies could not help but take phrase. The task's advertising and marketing essentially all of the time altered American advertising, and the monument has continued to be used over the years. For example, pix of the 4 Rushmore presidential pics had been depicted in a cool animated film created via manner of Walt Disney, and additionally in advertisements for severa beer providers.

While many have been disgusted, arguing that those corporations had been exploiting a country big sacred treasure, others asserted that using the mountain for business purposes should sincerely be endorsed and brought into attention an asset. The leader of Sioux Falls Argus claimed that those classified ads did now not defile the carving's emblematic have an impact on, however that as an alternative they best advanced national interest in paying go to to the net web page.

Regardless of Robinson and Borglum's private convictions, and what everyone else concept, too, the economic advertising and marketing advertising marketing campaign become a achievement. They received the funding that they needed to carve Mount Rushmore, and ultimately, the monuments although stays South Dakota's maximum worthwhile enchantment.

Chapter 11: Construction And Logistics

"His organization took lots of measurements on the model and then went as lots due to the fact the mountain and translated it times 12 to recreate the ones measurements at the mountain."

Amy Bracewell

In 1927, 4-hundred boys, males and females arrived inside the Black Hills in which they might spend the subsequent 14 years carving the pix of 4 United States presidents into the face of a mountain. The undertaking employed blacksmiths to make specialised drill bits and unique equipment. Tramway operators supervised the stable transporting of tool from the mountain's base all the way as tons as people operating loads of toes immoderate.

Fastened into bosun chairs, expert carvers and drillers prepared with jackhammers have been raised and reduced via other employees controlling the ones cranks and pulleys certainly with the aid of hand. Even this pastime end up tiresome and traumatic because if the winches had been tugged too unexpectedly or too speedy, whoever changed into sitting in the corresponding bosun chair might be launched into the mountain and pulled upwards at a risky speed, their face dragging inside the course of the tough granite alongside the manner.

As extra than ninety percent of Mount Rushmore become sculpted with explosives, powder men were hired to reduce dynamite sticks into particular measurements and then insert the explosives in crevices and holes to form the dense granite with powerful detonations. Borglum furthermore taught his employees a way for carving the granite that came to be called "the honeycomb method."

First, the human beings cited distinguished facial silhouettes and functions with crimson paint that indicated wherein and the manner deeply to carve. Then, they may jackhammer small holes into the granite in which they may later damage off sections of the honeycomb as wanted by means of using hammers and chisels. Finally, the employees might use a rotating diamond drill tip to easy and buff out the info.

Although the mission created exceptionally unsafe and threatening art work, notably, there has been not one unmarried worker fatality ultimately of the entire 14-12 months device. Nevertheless, it modified into no longer easy exertions. The humans sculpted Mount Rushmore all-yr-round. During the summer time they labored through particularly excessive temperatures due to the fact the solar beat down on them, and throughout the wintry weather, they battled snow and wind as they labored thru the frigid cold. In order to log their hours into the punch-clock that turned into positioned at the top of the mountain, the employee's needed to climb 700 stairs.

Once they arrived, metal cables three/eight inch thick were used to decrease the personnel down at some level within the mountain's massive 500-foot-face. Many said that they have got been honestly afraid of heights, however the $eight.00 an hour they earned become too pinnacle of a deal to skip up in the course of such devastating financial situations the last decade that have become the Great Depression.

Overseeing the entire assignment, Borglum determined that the extraordinary technique changed into to carve the mountain through specializing in one president at a time. Starting with Washington, he decided to vicinity the president's head on the cliff's tallest peak, which emerge as additionally the facet that faced maximum toward the the the the front. Next, Borglum should must cowl the peak with a plaster molding. A challenge that proved to be an epic challenge, it modified into despite the fact that no healthful for the prodigy who grow to be Borglum.

His devised a plan to construct a smaller model of the bust that might be scaled at a one-to-twelve ratio, this means that that one inch of the version changed into equivalent to 1 foot of the mountain. Looking down at the dimensions model from the top and middle of the top, Borglum have grow to be capable of quantify the appropriate distance from one characteristic to every other and the correct proportions of Washington's facial skills; i.E., ears, chin, cheekbones, nostril, and eyes. Then, the ones dimensions may be transferred onto the granite mountain.

On July four, 1930, a rite have become held to have an terrific time the of completion of Washington's bust. With over -thousand vacationers attending the event, Borglum stood proud as he located out that Mount Rushmore had in the end captured the extended-past due interest of the complete country. The morning after, but, proved to be even greater instrumental to the venture's reputation at the equal time as The New York Times recapped the event with the aid of using taking walks it due to the fact the the front internet internet web page story.

Interestingly, Washington's portrait became now not even completely finished on the time of the party. Borglum persisted to feature his finishing touches for each distinctive 11 months. In June of 1931, Borglum's group started to art work on Jefferson without the person himself. Borglum have turn out to be a real artist and a dreamer, and he did no longer want Mount Rushmore to dominate all of his time. After all, he had already created Jefferson's scale version and decided the bust's actual-lifestyles dimensions, and so he set sail for Europe that very month and located the assignment's each day operations into the arms of his reliable lieutenants.

While Borglum's group come to be geared up and expert, they ultimately had been confronted with a top notch problem that they couldn't manipulate on their very very own. It emerge as deliberate that Jefferson will be sculpted to the left of Washington, but that unique area inside the cliff proved heaps too broken and cracked to stand up to all the dynamite and jackhammering crucial to carve into the granite. Ultimately, Jefferson's head have come to be so misshapen that Borglum had no different desire however to barren region his real plans for the presidents' succession and changed into forced to begin all once more at the Jefferson bust that fall, this time setting it to the right of Washington.

Tragically although, the Great Depression started out out wreaking its maximum negative havoc all through the united states of a, and a congressional pause became positioned on the Rushmore project within the spring of 1932 so you can maintain capital. Devastated with the resource of way of the holdup, Borglum suffered financially proper alongside his human beings. After the Jefferson debacle, he and his own family had absolutely moved from Connecticut to South Dakota in order that he should supervise the operation onsite. But the investment that Congress pulled from the immediate had covered Borglum's paycheck, and this supposed that he might not get preserve of his compensation.

However, manner to Senator Norbeck, the delay may now not very last lengthy. The same spring Congress had introduced Rushmore to a standstill, it had additionally passed a bill that could allocate $three hundred million amongst each united states of america to be used for "unemployment remedy." Granted a $100 fifty,000 percentage, Norbeck turn out to be able to effectively employ South

Dakota's a part of the rest beneficial resource for Rushmore's resumption primarily based on the basis that its creation furnished properly over four hundred jobs. Resuming the carving of Thomas Jefferson that very fall, the crowning glory of the second presidential bust became celebrated without a doubt years later.

The halt of 1932 changed proper into a near to call, but Mount Rushmore's final touch become not however within the clear. In March of 1933, it become expected that more than sixteen million males and females have been out of work. While the monument definitely did provide masses of an entire lot-desired jobs in South Dakota, folks who resided in the state's east continued to be stricken by means of joblessness, homelessness, and hunger.

Predicting the risk that the Rushmore venture might quickly face each other interruption, Norbeck took motion yet again, and this time it modified into preemptive. In the midsummer of 1933, he petitioned the newly inaugurated President Roosevelt to sign a mandate that could deliver the National Park Service jurisdiction over the monument. Ultimately, this can require a part of the Park Service's price variety to be reserved for the task.

Although a clever one, Norbeck's approach may sooner or later purpose issues for Borglum inside the future because of wonderful situations covered in Roosevelt's directive. Essentially, the Mount Rushmore Association, which covered Borglum himself, emerge as now to reply to the Park Service and document all of the processes wherein they have been spending their allocated rate variety. It is recommended that Borglum threw multiple tantrums over the problem. Nevertheless, he have become in the end thankful to Norbeck due to the fact the actions he had taken ensured that the undertaking can be completed whilst no longer having to confront any further monetary emergencies along the way.

Borglum released the way of carving out the remaining two presidential busts in 1935. It fast have become easy, but, that his method to the complications with Jefferson's head had a consequential impact on the sculpting of Abraham Lincoln's. The trade in positions forced Borglum to transport every Lincoln and Theodore Roosevelt farther to the left, which in the end located Roosevelt into the mountain's internal most crevice. Lincoln modified into finished without impediment clearly two years later at some level in the summer time of 1937. And on September seventeenth of that equal 365 days, Lincoln's finishing touch grow to be celebrated on the same day because the a hundred and 50th birthday of the U.S. Constitution.

Artistically talking, Borglum taken into consideration the relocation rather best due to the fact the concave shape may additionally need to stand to emphasise the 3-dimensional complexity of his artwork; however realistically speaking, it created the very identical obstacles that had destroyed Jefferson's preliminary portrait in the first region. Borglum's crew have become forced to art work inner of the fissure in which they had to drill away a few 100 twenty feet of the cliff's floor to discover stone that come to be sturdy enough to live to inform the tale all the blasting and jackhammering. This obstacle delivered a severa-month get rid of inside the monument's creation.

Roosevelt's bust got here with other problems, too, as he turn out to be the handiest huge president who wore glasses a number of the 4. To conquer the predicament, Borglum constructed a crest across Roosevelt's nose and extra that reached each of his temples. Cleverly suggesting that those were the lines of eyeglass frames, Borglum relied on sightseers to fill within the blanks with their personal imaginations. Essentially, he created a actual-existence, large-sized optical phantasm.

Sadly, Gutzon Borglum did now not live to peer the finishing touch of his masterpiece. On March 6, 1941, the exquisite artist surpassed away at seventy three and left the undertaking's very last touches within the palms of his non-public son, Lincoln. In his mourning, Lincoln worked thru grief in order to complete his father's lifestyles work, but it become no a great deal an awful lot less than 4 months later that Congress declared the project finished whether it without a doubt modified into or not. The federal funding that had been allotted for Mount Rushmore's final touches had been redirected toward the battle that turned into to emerge as World War II.

Chapter 12: Controversies and Dissent

"Two adorable legends of the Lakotas is probably amazing topics for sculpturing-the Black Hills due to the fact the earth mother, and the story of the genesis of the tribe. Instead the face of a white guy is being stated at the face of a stone cliff inside the Black Hills. This lovely vicinity, of which the Lakota belief extra than a few other spot on the earth, brought about him the maximum ache and distress."

Luther Standing Bear

Mount Rushmore has end up known as the "Shrine of Democracy," but this interpretation of the monument is some distance from unanimous. Reflecting upon history, one ought to anticipate that web sites of outstanding sacred significance are simultaneously furthermore internet websites of large controversy.

In the case of Mount Rushmore, wherein one commercial enterprise organisation of humans is inspired and moved via the sculpture, each different isn't only offended, but additionally feels threatened, too. As it sits in the very center of the Black Hills, Mount Rushmore is greater to Native Americans than a trifling reminder of white American chauvinism inside the direction of their ancestors and appropriation in their land, it is, in truth, a flagrant and hurtful birthday party of it.

Dissent over the undertaking began out as soon as facts first spread that Doane Robinson and Gutzon Borglum were making plans to carve the faces of four

American presidents proper right into a mountain in the Black Hills. This preliminary opposition to Mount Rushmore had particularly come genuinely from white Americans, and it was the Lakotas, a Native American tribe inside the Black Hills', who had first supported it. However, the Lakotas concept it might be a grave mistake if Borglum have been outstanding to feature the faces of white guys on the mountain, specially given the truth that the Black Hills have been home to their tribe for hundreds of years earlier than whites even knew the continent itself existed.

Oglala Lakota Chief, Henry Standing Bear, met with Borglum in 1931 and asked him to reconsider the four snap shots he had selected. He counseled Borglum need to upload a fifth bust, considered one in every of "an Indian head" so that you can correct the monument and render it more legitimate.

Two years later, Luther Standing Bear, Henry's brother, expressed his very very own disapproval of Borglum's picks. He stated that " cute legends of the Lakotas might be tremendous topics for sculpturing the Black Hills as the earth mom, and the tale of the genesis of the tribe. Instead the face of a white guy is being noted at the face of a stone cliff within the Black Hills. This adorable location, of which the Lakota concept greater than a few different spot on the earth, prompted him the most pain and distress."

Sadly, the Lakota Standing Bear brothers did no longer apprehend that

Borglum may have in no manner even contemplated the mere idea of sculpting a Lakota determine next to the white presidents on Mount Rushmore or on any mountain face for that depend. Despite the reality that Borglum publically displayed himself as an suggest for the "noble" Native American, in his private existence he have end up an active racist or maybe a member of the Ku Klux Klan.

It is rumored that it turned into the Borglum family's racist sentiments that stirred the battle of words among Lincoln Borglum and their artist assistant, Korczak Ziolkowski. It is not any twist of fate that when Ziolkowski surrender the Rushmore project that he spark off to begin carving up each different mountain nearby. Per the request of Henry Standing Bear,

Ziolkowski started out the massive sculpture of Crazy Horse, a venture that remains unfinished to in the interim.

It isn't always any mystery that the first half of the 20 th century have become a period of splendid ache and strain for almost all of Native Americans. For example, any and all conventional Native American religions were unlawful for the tribes to workout until the 1933 passing of the Taft-Howard Act. Additionally, earlier than the act gave tribal governments autonomy over their very non-public humans, america Office of Indian Affairs oversaw and strictly regulated Native American societies and their sports activities activities. It changed into no longer for some exclusive thirty years that Native Americans started out to see any similarly development regarding the civil rights and the sovereignty they want to have had all along as an independent u . S . A ..

During the 1960s, white American lifestyle modified into falling apart, changing, and starting to reorganize. Recognizing the possibility accessible, a tough and rapid of Native Americans began out out the American Indian Movement, or AIM, in 1968. When thinking about in which to begin their demonstrations, no individual have to argue that each figuratively and in reality there was no big image of the oppression that that they had prolonged suffered than Mount Rushmore. The monument end up an unadulterated example of white America's disrespect for the Native American and whole refusal to understand Native American historic contributions or significance.

Between Natives Americans and whites, conflict regarding everything of the Black Hills predates even the mid-nineteenth century. The civil rights moves of the Sixties provided AIM with a fantastic canvas to begin expressing their grievances, not simplest because it have turn out to be a time of revolution for each underrepresented organization of human beings, however moreover because of the fact white American modified into truly beginning to pay attention. An powerful and militant commercial enterprise company, AIM utilized various strategies that could all the time modify the nation's perspective of Mount Rushmore.

Throughout the 1970s, Native American protestors took whole control of the memorial, marching for numerous days at a time. Targeting unique injustices, they first raised country wide attention for the reality that america federal authorities had snubbed Native American requests that all Pine Ridge land be once more to them. The region had been seized all through World War II through the usage of the U.S. Army for schooling capabilities, and even though they had been promised that they may regain manage of the land after the conflict ended, the U.S. Authorities broke its word, and as a substitute, protected Pine Ridge inside the jurisdiction of Badlands National Park.

Second, AIM protestors proclaimed their rightful possession of the Lakota

Black Hills. In an instance that lasted for 3 months, on August 23 hundreds of Lakota protestors commenced their career of Mount Rushmore. The demonstration gained the eye of the country wide press, however the way wherein the click said at the state of affairs became whatever however unbiased.

Reporters wrote in their outright condemnation of AIM's strategies. One article by way of the use of the use of the Los Angeles Herald Examiner found a story that study, "Rushmore brings out the superb in human beings…. Rushmore did now not perform the great in the ones humans. Like the minority radicals everywhere, not anything seems to encourage decency or correct. They had been only inquisitive about destruction. Kooks are kooks the world over."

Regardless of the way non violent and diplomatic AIM needed to begin with tried to be, the pix allotted thru the clicking offering the congregation of hundreds of Native Americans marching on the memorial created fear and countrywide panic amongst whites all for the duration of the u . S .. White vacationers stopped journeying the website online, and those who did have been exceptional there to hassle Native American protestors and file proceedings. White America taken into consideration the Lakota demonstrations to be an assault on public place, no matter the reality that that they had definitely as an lousy lot right as all people else to be there if no longer more so. The press' outright refusal to document that there has been any legitimacy to Native American court cases outraged AIM contributors.

Hundreds of editorials have been discovered in American newspapers claiming that the protestors have been radicalized and violent, regardless of the reality that on the time they have been no longer. Such blatant mendacity started out to have its impact, and the impact come to be that protestors ultimately did grow to be certainly radicalized. For example, one AIM demonstrator gave a extended speech in which he stated, "Perhaps in advance than it's far too overdue, the relaxation of the Nation will awaken to the greatness of our way of life, and all guys can be brothers. If not, then we're able to all succumb to finish annihilation at the hand of the white man's greed and shortage of statistics."

Conflict regarding Mount Rushmore and who want to rightfully claim ownership of the Black Hills endured via the rest of the twentieth century, and eventually, the Lakotas were granted their day in court. In what no matter the truth that remains the maximum drawn-out litigation in United States records, in 1980 Native Americans all around the united states of the us had been subsequently vindicated thru the U.S. Supreme Court. For the illegal seizure of the Black Hills in 1877, the Court dominated that the federal authorities owed the Lakota tribe beneficiant repayment, one that grew to over $350 million dollars through manner of 1990.

Every twelve months, over 3 million Americans tour to Mount Rushmore to gaze upon the four faces of their cherished presidents. The carving inspires people, it makes them enjoy proud, confident, and effective. But no longer simply each person feels this manner while searching up on the monument; and maximum in all likelihood, the faces of folks who do experience this manner are white faces and this is why preserving that any public internet website is come what may additionally additionally divine or sacred is intrinsically controversial. Something cannot be universally sacred if it lifts up one organization of people and but oppresses some other.

Chapter 13: Monumental Meaning

"The herbal marvels of the West compensated for America's lack of antique cities, [and] aristocratic traditions."

Despite controversy and dissent, one cannot argue with the patriotic power of Mount Rushmore. The monument is exempt from polarized political ideologies, and instead, it no longer only celebrates them, but has historically been utilized by leaders to unite them. For example, the photo of Mount Rushmore changed into hired to rally Americans in opposition to Communism at a few stage inside the Cold War. In 1952, Drew Pearson stood in front of the mountain as he recommended the united states to renew their American patriotism and placed their believe in the presidential administration.

A patriotic icon, in the faces of Mount Rushmore there is largely a political fluidity. It certainly can't be married to any singular set of ideological thoughts. Nevertheless, the monument is an prolonged way from sacred because it fuses religious sentiments with employer profiteering. Its very private creators, Robinson and Borglum, paraded Mount Rushmore's capability to both be lucrative and concurrently provide nationalistic sentiment and devotion.

However, maximum sociologists agree that the monument isn't always on my own on this regard. Like all patriotic and religious shrines regarded for inspiring pilgrimage, Mount Rushmore is really as masses in the commercial organization of tourism as they'll be; because of this, sociologists are even though amazed via the truth that many Americans have no longer began to overcome their terrible thoughts-set regarding any commercialization of the monument.

An apparent reason for such large aversion is the manner wherein Mount Rushmore has been used for political campaigning or maybe the advertising and marketing of beer and special merchandise. But possibly what has left the greatest awful have an effect on on the general public is the range of orientation or propaganda movies which have been created for the mountain considering the truth that 1965. These films are portrayed as ancient, informational works, innocently meant to train the overall public approximately the monument's information and the manner of its creation.

However, most of its visitors apprehend that the filmmakers' had the underlying cause to basically indoctrinate Americans. The Mount Rushmore National Memorial management has been identified to strain vacationers into attending the screenings of these movies inside the monument's tourist's middle. Furthermore, earlier than travelers even lay eyes on the mountain, rangers for the National Park Service train them to include the propaganda film into their schedule for the day, or maybe the monument's found out and on-line literature suggest the movies, too.

The orientation film has been up to date on three separate activities, and a complete evaluation of every films' tropes and anthems, which fairly exchange whenever a new movie is released, well-known the blatant institutional efforts to essentially manufacture the mountain's this means that. The movies portray a kind of cultural concord that doesn't exist in truth, and this brotherly love is advertised without the slightest popularity for any of america' preceding sports activities that have been each unethical and violent.

In an evaluation completed through renown communication university college students, Robert Hariman and John Louis Lucaities wrote that with the useful resource of the use of manipulative methods the films try and normalize the "matrices of privilege," which embody "imperialism, expansionism," and the supremacy of whites and the Christian religion.

In 1964, Charles W. Nauman sent his script for an orientation film to the Mount Rushmore National Memorial Society. In his personal phrases, Nauman said that the reason of the film changed into to "report and interpret the statistics and the ideals embodied at Mount Rushmore Memorial." Simply titled, "Mount Rushmore," the movie blends the monument's figurative values with the skills of its creator, Gutzon Borglum. And this conflation become powered by the use of the sculptor's notions of American creativity and innovation.

During Mount Rushmore's carving, Borglum expected that the mountain might likely now not only memorialize American expansionism, however that it would even function a shrine commemorating imperialism. What is now taken into consideration to be honestly an offensive ideology, it become one that modified into significantly commonplace at that factor. The United States emerge as now not only tormented by the Great Depression, however it had additionally clearly pop out of World War I. Historian Michael Schudson wrote that Americans shared a "worry of anarchism, socialism, and bolshevism, plus state of affairs about the want to Americanize immigrants [were] motives for a renewed interest in the

Constitution and all topics American inside the Twenties and '30s."

Although it become seemed that the Native American country nearly unanimously disapproved of Mount Rushmore, their condemnation of the monument became not publically voiced until the overdue Nineteen Sixties, and it became no longer visibly set up till they occupied the mountain at a few level within the 1970s. Nevertheless, the primary Rushmore-propaganda filmmakers identified the shape of discernment that they might need to workout; and as a cease result, they selected to exclude any mention that, via his creation of the monument, Borglum himself have turn out to be essentially reminiscent of white supremacy and imperialism.

The starting of the film explains how Borglum first gained his revel in with developing big sculptures with the aid of planning to carve Georgia's Stone Mountain. There are fourteen pix in state-of-the-art that depict numerous levels of Stone Mountain's improvement, and however, there is not a unmarried reference to Borglum becoming a member of the Ku Klux Klan in the course of that factor. The filmmakers do now not even factor out how disastrously the project ended.

Borglum emerge as not merely most effective a passive member of the KKK, he had simply named the racist employer as his most influential motivation for running on Stone Mountain in the first vicinity. Borglum desired to create "a powerful political pressure" out of the KKK that might be "strong enough to make countrywide insurance." Skipping over such interesting and valuable historic facts, the orientation movie truely states that Borglum's "artwork have become in fundamental phrases and newly American," and that the person himself "grow to be an intensely nationalistic and patriotic artist."

Borglum's carving made a everlasting exchange both at the Black Hills' panorama and the manner wherein regular Americans diagnosed themselves and their citizenship. However, the correct countrywide identity that Borglum carved into Mount Rushmore has modified loads over the years that it has but to be exactly diagnosed in and of itself.

In 1925, Borglum stated that the monument modified into intended to have amusing America's independence from Great Britain within the Revolutionary War, to honor the "Empire Builders," and commemorate "the Louisiana Purchase, [and] the securing of Oregon, Texas, California, Alaska and Panama." He went directly to provide an explanation for that the ones are the motives he selected the presidents that he did for the mountain.

Borglum decided on George Washington to symbolize the dominion's founding and its rich, infinite future. However, he ignored to make any point out of Washington's presidential farewell cope with, wherein he expressed his uncertainty regarding the Revolutionary War's outcome. The first president had ended this speech with a assertion expressing the he couldn't determine whether or no longer or not or not he "considered [America's independence] as a blessing or a curse."

Thomas Jefferson modified into decided on to symbolize the Louisiana Purchase, however Borglum in no manner stated the loads of lots of Native Americans who paid for American expansionism with their lives and cultures. Or moreover, that the Louisiana Purchase basically stole the Black Hills from the Lakotas. Abraham Lincoln become selected to represent American cohesion, however Borglum ignored the reality that 1/2 of the us desired so passionately to secede throughout Lincoln's presidency that they went to war over it.

And in the long run, Theodore Roosevelt become selected to symbolize progressiveness, contemporary-day innovation, and "a new diploma of [American] attention," but Borglum by no means stated the truth that Roosevelt had time and again been on file for ignoring the exertions crimes of the very wealthy and the manner wherein they exploited their personal personnel who belonged to the strolling-elegance of Americans.

Chapter 14: Modern Rushmore

"I have become appalled at the sight of the flag pole atop the Mt. Rushmore carving. It appears to me that this is going too far with the Bicentennial challenge remember. To me, the sight of this flag pole is a desecration of the majestic paintings of the Mt. Rushmore carving."

Anonymous Mount Rushmore tourist

Every one year, nearly three million humans make their pilgrimage to South Dakota at the way to look with their very private eyes the significant six-tale busts of four hundreds-loved American presidents. The twelve months after the assaults of Sept. 11, those visitor numbers rose through an great 15 percent. Since then, one of the internet web page's excellent days for attendance changed into on October 31, 2016, the seventy fifth anniversary of Mount Rushmore's of completion. The day modified into mainly famous because it become moreover the one hundredth birthday of the National Park Service.

While one can also anticipate that the time had handed long in the beyond for controversy and dissent concerning Mount Rushmore, such an assumption could not be further from the truth. After all, the monument itself have come to be speculated to spark strong and passionate responses from its web site traffic, and as a end result, National Park Services is accountable for regulating the huge collection of effects and zealous reactions that Mount Rushmore creates.

For instance, in 1976, the American flag have become located at the pinnacle of Mount Rushmore to commemorate the us of the usa's Bicentennial birthday, and this smooth act caused this type of polarized but complicated dispute, and it grow to be one that many human beings struggled to even recognise. National Park Service idea that hoisting the American flag at the mountain's top is probably no longer anything extra than the nice gesture. Nevertheless, it acquired a form of backlash that no one need to have anticipated. After all, who may assume that such a whole lot of humans may additionally want to find out the American flag on top of an American monument to be offensive? But it genuinely so took place that at the very day the flag changed into raised, NPS superintendent Harvey

Wickware began out compiling a collection of 1 objection after any other.

One traveler complained that the flag have become a distraction from the "smooth majesty of the sculpture itself." An architect who specialised in panorama despatched a letter to NPS director Gary Eberhardt and wrote that he turned into upset "such defacing of a rustic wide monument changed into certainly perpetrated with the beneficial useful resource of the National Park Service itself." He even criticized its very aesthetics, calling the sight more than a mere "distraction," however that it became "in very, very bad flavor."

At first, the NPS defended its desire to elevate the flag at the pinnacle of

Mount Rushmore, primarily based at the reasoning that it simplest made revel in to elevate it on America's Bicentennial birthday because it have become a number one function of American patriotism. But much less than steady with week later, superintendent Wickware ordered the flag be removed because of the NPS's notion that the problem "become beginning to have the overtones of a trouble." For folks who cherished the flag, Wickware tried to sooth the ones capability court cases putting forward that its decreasing "should in no intense way have an effect on our spirits in this Bicentennial year."

But of course, his try to appease one group simplest incited some distinctive. Letters of latest courtroom instances quick got here pouring in. Particularly, the Mount Rushmore National Memorial Service obtained the protest of 1 concerned citizen who said, "Personally I can't apprehend how some people can determine that the flag must now not be there in reality will we have to pay attention to the ones few? Why are Communists allowed to dictate in our Black Hills?" Other lawsuits said that the NPS easily reduced the American flag, and but, turn out to be inclined to allow buddies of the International Society for Krishna Consciousness to panhandle inside the the front of the monument.

In defense of its refusal to eliminate the so-known as "beggars" from the website, Rushmore's nearby director Lynn Thompson argued that that beneath the First Amendment, individuals of the Hare Krishna company had every right to be there thinking about the fact that they represent a religious organisation. Nevertheless, many Americans interpreted this low-priced and constitutional explanation as even though the federal authorities modified into in a few form of cahoots with remote places and radical spiritual extremists.

More presently, attempts to renovate the vacationer net net web page, that could incorporate erecting an up to date traveller's center, gift stores, administrative centers, and the paving of a modern day parking zone, have been contested. In particular, the Sierra Club argued that any new inclinations at the net net web page might be an absolute desecration as they might genuinely be observed via the use of the domineering and suffocating entities of bureaucracy. Its contributors have even warned that they might report a lawsuit over the trouble. These forms of disputes over Mount Rushmore have become so normalized that the NPS not simplest expects them, however they now robotically educate their personnel to manipulate them.

Despite court docket instances, the MRNMS has controlled to put in contemporary-day-day generation at Mount Rushmore. For example, the mountain is lighted each middle of the night to decorate the midnight view for visitors who need to gaze upon the monument after darkish. However, it changed into positioned that pleasant forms of illumination can affect herbal depend huge range. It draws in moths and exceptional nocturnal creatures, so the employer finished up to date LED lighting fixtures in 2015 to reduce any undesirable outcomes.

Other efforts to maintain the monument include a three-D digital scanner that has assessed the mountain inner-out, reaching an accuracy this is anticipated to be off no extra than a single centimeter. This comprehensive generation have end up created in the event that a few sort of herbal catastrophe wreaked havoc upon Mount Rushmore. Basically, due to the reality the monument become sculpted, Borglum had ordered his personnel to seal every little crack with a concoction of granite dirt and linseed oil.

www.ingramcontent.com/pod-product-compliance
Lightning Source LLC
Chambersburg PA
CBHW071444080526
44587CB00014B/1987